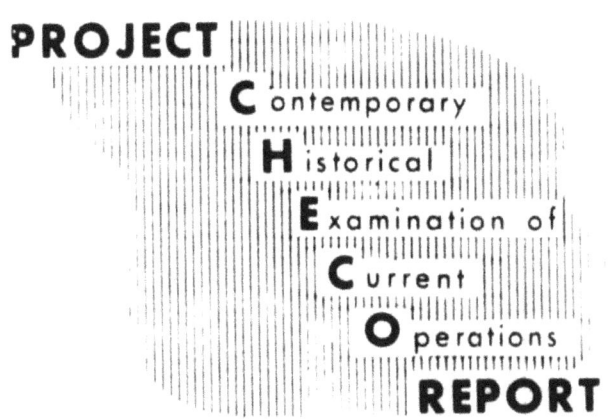

RANCH HAND: HERBICIDE OPERATIONS IN SEA

13 JULY 1971

HQ PACAF

Directorate of Operations Analysis
CHECO/CORONA HARVEST DIVISION

Prepared by:

CAPT. JAMES R. CLARY

Project CHECO 7th AF, DOAC

PROJECT CHECO REPORTS

The counterinsurgency and unconventional warfare environment of Southeast Asia has resulted in the employment of USAF airpower to meet a multitude of requirements. The varied applications of airpower have involved the full spectrum of USAF aerospace vehicles, support equipment, and manpower. As a result, there has been an accumulation of operational data and experiences that, as a priority, must be collected, documented, and analyzed as to current and future impact upon USAF policies, concepts, and doctrine.

Fortunately, the value of collecting and documenting our SEA experiences was recognized at an early date. In 1962, Hq USAF directed CINCPACAF to establish an activity that would be primarily responsive to Air Staff requirements and direction, and would provide timely and analytical studies of USAF combat operations in SEA.

Project CHECO, an acronym for Contemporary Historical Examination of Current Operations, was established to meet this Air Staff requirement. Managed by Hq PACAF, with elements at Hq 7AF and 7AF/13AF, Project CHECO provides a scholarly, "on-going" historical examination, documentation, and reporting on USAF policies, concepts, and doctrine in PACOM. This CHECO report is part of the overall documentation and examination which is being accomplished. It is an authentic source for an assessment of the effectiveness of USAF airpower in PACOM when used in proper context. The reader must view the study in relation to the events and circumstances at the time of its preparation--recognizing that it was prepared on a contemporary basis which restricted perspective and that the author's research was limited to records available within his local headquarters area.

ERNEST C. HARDIN, JR., Major General, USAF
Chief of Staff

REPLY TO
ATTN OF: DOAD

13 July 1971

Project CHECO Report, "Ranch Hand: Herbicide Operations in SEA" (U)

SEE DISTRIBUTION PAGE

1. Attached is a SECRET NOFORN document. It shall be transported, stored, safeguarded, and accounted for in accordance with applicable security directives. SPECIAL HANDLING REQUIRED, NOT RELEASABLE TO FOREIGN NATIONALS. The information contained in this document will not be disclosed to foreign nations or their representatives. Retain or destroy in accordance with AFR 205-1. Do not return.

2. This letter does not contain classified information and may be declassified if attachment is removed from it.

FOR THE COMMANDER IN CHIEF

MAURICE L. GRIFFITH, Colonel, USAF   1 Atch
Chief, CHECO/CORONA HARVEST Division   Proj CHECO Rprt (S/NF), 13 Jul 71
Directorate of Operations Analysis
DCS/Operations

DISTRIBUTION LIST

1. SECRETARY OF THE AIR FORCE

    a. SAFAA 1
    b. SAFLL 1
    c. SAFOI 2
    d. SAFUS 1

2. HEADQUARTERS USAF

    a. AFNB 1

    b. AFCCS
        (1) AFCCSSA 1
        (2) AFCVC 1
        (3) AFCAV 1
        (4) AFCHO 2

    c. AFCSA
        (1) AFCSAG 1
        (2) AFCSAMI 1

    d. AFOA 1

    e. AFIGO
        (1) OSIIAP 3
        (2) IGS 1

    f. AFSG 1

    g. AFNIATC 5

    h. AFAAC 1
        (1) AFACMI 1

    i. AFODC
        (1) AFPRC 1
        (2) AFPRE 1
        (3) AFPRM 1

    j. AFPDC
        (1) AFDPW 1

    k. AFRD
        (1) AFRDP 1
        (2) AFRDQ 1
        (3) AFRDQPC 1
        (4) AFRDR 1
        (5) AFRDQL 1

    l. AFSDC
        (1) AFSLP 1
        (2) AFSME 1
        (3) AFSMS 1
        (4) AFSSS 1
        (5) AFSTP 1

    m. AFTAC 1

    n. AFXO 1
        (1) AFXOB 1
        (2) AFXOD 1
        (3) AFXODC 1
        (4) AFXODD 1
        (5) AFXODL 1
        (6) AFXOOAB 1
        (7) AFXOSL 1
        (8) AFXOOSN 1
        (9) AFXOOSO 1
        (10) AFXOOSS 1
        (11) AFXOOSV 1
        (12) AFXOOTR 1
        (13) AFXOOTW 1
        (14) AFXOOTZ 1
        (15) AF/XOX 6
        (16) AFXOXXG 1

3. MAJOR COMMAND

   a. TAC

      (1) HEADQUARTERS
         (a) DO. 1
         (b) XP. 1
         (c) DOCC. 1
         (d) DREA. 1
         (e) IN. 1

      (2) AIR FORCES
         (a) 12AF
            1. DOO. 1
            2. IN 1
         (b) 19AF(IN). 1
         (c) USAFSOF(DO) 1

      (3) WINGS
         (a) 1SOW(DOI) 1
         (b) 23TFW(DOI). 1
         (c) 27TRW(DOI). 1
         (d) 33TFW(DOI). 1
         (e) 64TAW(DOI). 1
         (f) 67TRW(DOI). 1
         (g) 75TRW(DOI). 1
         (h) 316TAW(DOX) 1
         (i) 363TRW(DOI) 1
         (j) 464TFW(DOI) 1
         (k) 474TFW(DOI) 1
         (l) 479TFW(DOI) 1
         (m) 516TAW(DOX) 1
         (n) 4403TFW(DOI). . . . 1
         (o) 58TAC FTR TNG WG. . 1
         (p) 354TFW(DOI) 1
         (q) 60MAWG(DOOXI) . . . 1

      (4) TAC CENTERS, SCHOOLS
         (a) USAFTAWC(DRA) . . . 1
         (b) USAFTFWC(DRA) . . . 1
         (c) USAFAGOS(EDA) . . . 1

   b. SAC

      (1) HEADQUARTERS
         (a) DOX 1
         (b) XPX 1
         (c) DM. 1
         (d) IN. 1
         (e) NR. 1
         (f) HO. 1

      (2) AIR FORCES
         (a) 2AF(INCS) 1
         (b) 8AF(DOA). 2
         (c) 15AF(INCE). 1

   c. MAC

      (1) HEADQUARTERS
         (a) DOI 1
         (b) DOO 1
         (c) CSEH. 1
         (d) MACOA 1

      (2) MAC SERVICES
         (a) AWS(HO) 1
         (b) ARRS(XP) 1
         (c) ACGS(CGO) 1

   d. ADC

      (1) HEADQUARTERS
         (a) DO. 1
         (b) DOT 1
         (c) XPC 1

      (2) AIR DIVISIONS
         (a) 25AD(DOI) 1
         (b) 23AD(DOI) 1
         (c) 20AD(DOI) 1

   e. ATC
      (1) DOSPI 1

f. AFLC

   (1) HEADQUARTERS
      (a) XOX 1

g. AFSC

   (1) HEADQUARTERS
      (a) XRP 1
      (b) XRLW. 1
      (c) SAMSO(XRS). 1
      (d) SDA 1
      (e) CSH 1
      (f) ASD(RWST) 1
      (g) ESD(XO) 1
      (h) RADC(DCTL). 1
      (i) ADTC(CCN) 1
      (j) ADTC(SSLT). 1
      (k) ESD(YW) 1
      (l) AFATL(DL) 1

h. USAFSS

   (1) HEADQUARTERS
      (a) AFSCC(SUR). 2

   (2) SUBORDINATE UNITS
      (a) Eur Scty Rgn(OPD-P) . 1
      (b) 6940 Scty Wg(OOD) . . 1

i. AAC

   (1) HEADQUARTERS
      (a) ALDOC-A 1

j. USAFSO

   (1) HEADQUARTERS
      (a) CSH 1

k. PACAF

   (1) HEADQUARTERS
      (a) DP 1
      (b) IN 1
      (c) XP 2
      (d) CSH. 1
      (e) DOAD 6
      (f) DC 1
      (g) DM 1

   (2) AIR FORCES
      (a) 5AF
         1. CSH 1
         2. XP. 1
         3. DO. 1
      (b) Det 8, ASD(DOASD). . 1
      (c) 7AF
         1. DO. 1
         2. IN. 1
         3. XP. 1
         4. DOCT. 1
         5. DOAC. 2
      (d) 13AF
         1. CSH 1
      (e) 7/13AF(CHECO). . . . 1

   (3) AIR DIVISIONS
      (a) 313AD(DOI) 1
      (b) 314AD(XOP) 2
      (c) 327AD
         1. IN. 1
      (d) 834AD(DO). 2

        (4) WINGS
            (a) 8TFW(DOEA) 1
            (b) 12TFW(DOIN) 1
            (c) 56SOW(WHD) 1
            (d) 366TFW(DO) 1
            (e) 388TFW(DO) 1
            (f) 405TFW(DOEA) 1
            (g) 432TRW(DOI) 1
            (h) 460TRW(DOI) 1
            (i) 475TFW(DCO) 1
            (j) 1st Test Sq(A) 1

        (5) OTHER UNITS
            (a) Task Force ALPHA(IN) . . 1
            (b) 504TASG(DO) 1
            (c) Air Force Advisory Gp. . 1

1. USAFE

        (1) HEADQUARTERS
            (a) DOA. 1
            (b) DOLO 1
            (c) DOO. 1
            (d) XDC. 1

        (2) AIR FORCES
            (a) 3AF(DO) 2
            (b) 16AF(DO) 1
            (c) 17AF(IN) 1

        (3) WINGS
            (a) 36TFW(DCOID) 1
            (b) 50TFW(DOA) 1
            (c) 20TFW(DOI) 1
            (d) 401TFW(DCOI) 1
            (e) 513TAW(DOI) 1

4. SEPARATE OPERATING AGENCIES
    a. ACIC(DOP) 2
    b. AFRES(XP) 2
    c. AU
        1. ACSC-SA 1
        2. AUL(SE)-69-108 2
        3. ASI(ASD-1) 1
        4. ASI(HOA) 2
    d. ANALYTIC SERVICES, INC . 1
    e. USAFA
        1. DFH 1
    f. AFAG(THAILAND) 1

5. MILITARY DEPARTMENTS, UNIFIED AND SPECIFIED COMMANDS, AND JOINT STAFFS

    a. COMUSJAPAN 1
    b. CINCPAC (SAG). 1
    c. CINCPAC (J301) 1
    d. CINCPACFLT (Code 321). 1
    e. COMUSKOREA (ATTN: J-3) 1
    f. COMUSMACTHAI 1
    g. COMUSMACV (TSCO) 1
    h. COMUSTDC (J3) 1
    i. USCINCEUR (ECJB) 1
    j. USCINCSO (DCC) 1
    k. CINCLANT (N31) 1
    l. CHIEF, NAVAL OPERATIONS. 1
    m. COMMANDANT, MARINE CORPS (ABQ) 1
    n. CINCONAD (CHSV-M). 1
    o. DEPARTMENT OF THE ARMY (TAGO). 1
    p. JOINT CHIEFS OF STAFF (J3RR&A) 1
    q. JSTPS. 1
    r. SECRETARY OF DEFENSE (OASD/SA) 1
    s. CINCSTRIKE (STRJ-3). 1
    t. CINCAL (HIST). 1
    u. MAAG-CHINA/AF Section (MGAF-O) 1
    v. HQ ALLIED FORCES NORTHERN EUROPE (U.S. DOCUMENTS OFFICE) 1
    w. USMACV (MACJ031) 1

6. SCHOOLS

    a. Senior USAF Representative, National War College 1
    b. Senior USAF Representative, Armed Forces Staff College 1
    c. Senior USAF Rep, Industrial College of the Armed Forces. 1
    d. Senior USAF Representative, Naval Amphibious School. 1
    e. Senior USAF Rep, U.S. Marine Corps Education Center. 1
    f. Senior USAF Representative, U.S. Naval War College 1
    g. Senior USAF Representative, U.S. Army War College. 1
    h. Senior USAF Rep, U.S. Army C&G Staff College 1
    i. Senior USAF Representative, U.S. Army Infantry School. 1
    j. Senior USAF Rep, U.S. Army JFK Center for Special Warfare. . . . 1
    k. Senior USAF Representative, U.S. Army Field Artillery School . . 1
    l. Senior USAF Representative, U.S. Liaison Office. 1

7. SPECIAL

    a. The RAND Corporation 1
    b. U.S. Air Attache, Vientiane. 1

TABLE OF CONTENTS

	Page
PREFACE	xi
CHAPTER I - MISSION AND TACTICS	1
CHAPTER II - HERBICIDE REVIEW, 1961-1967	6
CHAPTER III - HERBICIDE OPERATIONS, 1967-1971	17
CHAPTER IV - BIOLOGICAL ASPECTS OF HERBICIDE	33
EFFECTS OF DEFOLIATION	34
Soils	36
Botanical Considerations - Mangrove Forest	38
Botanical Considerations - Semideciduous Forest	39
Animals	40
APPENDIX A - BIOLOGICAL/ECOLOGICAL EFFECTS OF HERBICIDES	41
APPENDIX B - RANCH HAND SORTIES (HERBICIDE, INSECTICIDE, LEAFLET) GALLONS OF HERBICIDE DISPENSED AND AIRCRAFT ASSIGNED TO RANCH HAND	72
APPENDIX C - HERBICIDE PROJECTS, ALL CORPS, 1967-1971	78
APPENDIX D - HERBICIDE SORTIES IN LAOS, 1965-1969	105
FOOTNOTES	
CHAPTER I	107
CHAPTER II	107
CHAPTER III	111
CHAPTER IV	114
GLOSSARY	117
RESEARCH NOTE	121

FIGURES   Follows Page

1. (U) Photo: "Patches" xiii
2. (U) Photo: Seven-Aircraft Defoliation Mission   2
3. (U) Photo: Ranch Hand Aircraft in Formation   4
4. (C) SVN Crop Destruction Missions, Jan 65-Feb 71.......   76
5. (C) SVN Defoliation Missions, Jan 65-Feb 71   76
6. (U) SVN Provinces and Military Regions   76

PREFACE

This is the final history of herbicide operations in Southeast Asia, code named Trail Dust. But, it is more the story of a group of dedicated men, with an esprit de corps usually found only in fighter outfits. These men flew C-123 aircraft on missions throughout Southeast Asia. Although they were assigned to a variety of organizations, they retained the code name of their unit, "Ranch Hand," throughout their nine years of operation.

From the moment of its inception "Ranch Hand" was a controversial unit. The herbicide and defoliation mission was to attack enemy strongholds throughout SEA.

Critics were abundant, pointing out failures to accomplish any clear-cut objectives. The proponents cited the many roads cleared to prevent ambush attempts, the greater visibility made available to our planes to watch enemy movement, the tons of food made inaccessible to the enemy, and the serious logistic problems encountered by the enemy when he was denied the plush green valleys and had to plant in isolated areas and along steep hillsides. But whether you were a critic or an advocate of Ranch Hand, you had to admire its crewmembers and the legend they left for posterity: a legend cherished by its members and all those who were fortunate enough to be associated with the unit.

Few will forget the resounding cheers heard in many of the officers' clubs throughout Vietnam, "Let's hear it for the Ranch!" For over nine years this colorful outfit proudly wore their cowboy hats, berets, and finally their purple scarves and party suits for all occasions.

From 1965 on the unit's pride was manifested in the wearing of the purple scarf. The scarf was presented to the Ranch by then Premier Nguyen Cao Ky after he flew with them on target. Premier Ky took off his own scarf and presented it to the aircraft commander and told him, "These are your colors, wear them with pride." Wear it they did. It was worn at all occasions, and some even wore it under their shade 1505 uniforms when they rotated. The scarf was subsequently awarded only to those members who flew on target. It became a much sought-after award and those who flew with the Ranch on target knew they had earned their scarf.

The Purple Heart was also nearly synonymous with the name of this unit. The aircraft were flown low and slow over enemy territory which consisted of triple canopy jungle, lush valleys and steep mountains. Danger was frequent in the unit's experience.

The UC-123 Provider (first the UC-123B, followed by the jet modified UC-123K) aircraft was ideally suited for this mission, for many times it absorbed extensive battle damage and yet brought the crew back safely. During its nine year history Ranch aircraft sustained over 7,000 hits from enemy ground fire, a mere fraction of the ground fire aimed at them, which included small arms, automatic weapons, and .50 caliber. It was not unusual for an aircraft to sustain more than 30 hits on a single mission, have several controls and instruments disabled, and yet limp home. It was a great credit to the crews and to the ruggedness of the planes that few aircraft were lost. One particular aircraft, affectionately called "Patches," sustained over 600 hits and earned consideration for placement in the Air Force Museum at Wright-Patterson Air Force Base, Ohio. This aircraft was the only C-123 to fly around the world. At the time of this report "Patches" was still flying spray missions, now as a "Bug Bird" dispensing insecticide in the Vietnam malaria control program.

Since the Trail Dust mission was unique, tactics had to be designed on a trial and error basis to provide for maximum surprise and concealment. With the development of new tactics and techniques also developed a colorful terminology used during the missions. Terms such as "Leaving the corral" (the formation is leaving the parking area); "Saddle up" (all aircraft get into formation); and "Take it down, Cowboys" (descend to target altitude) all added more color to the Ranch Hand lore.

This unit became one of the most decorated flying outfits in Southeast Asia during its nine years of operation. Ranch awards included numerous Silver Stars, Distinguished Flying Crosses, Air Medals, Vietnamese Air Force (VNAF) Wings, Vietnamese Medals of Honor, Vietnamese Campaign Ribbons and Presidential Unit Citations--not to mention the Purple Heart.[1]

This, then, is the story of the Ranch, and it may help to answer the question "Where have all the Ranch Hands gone?"

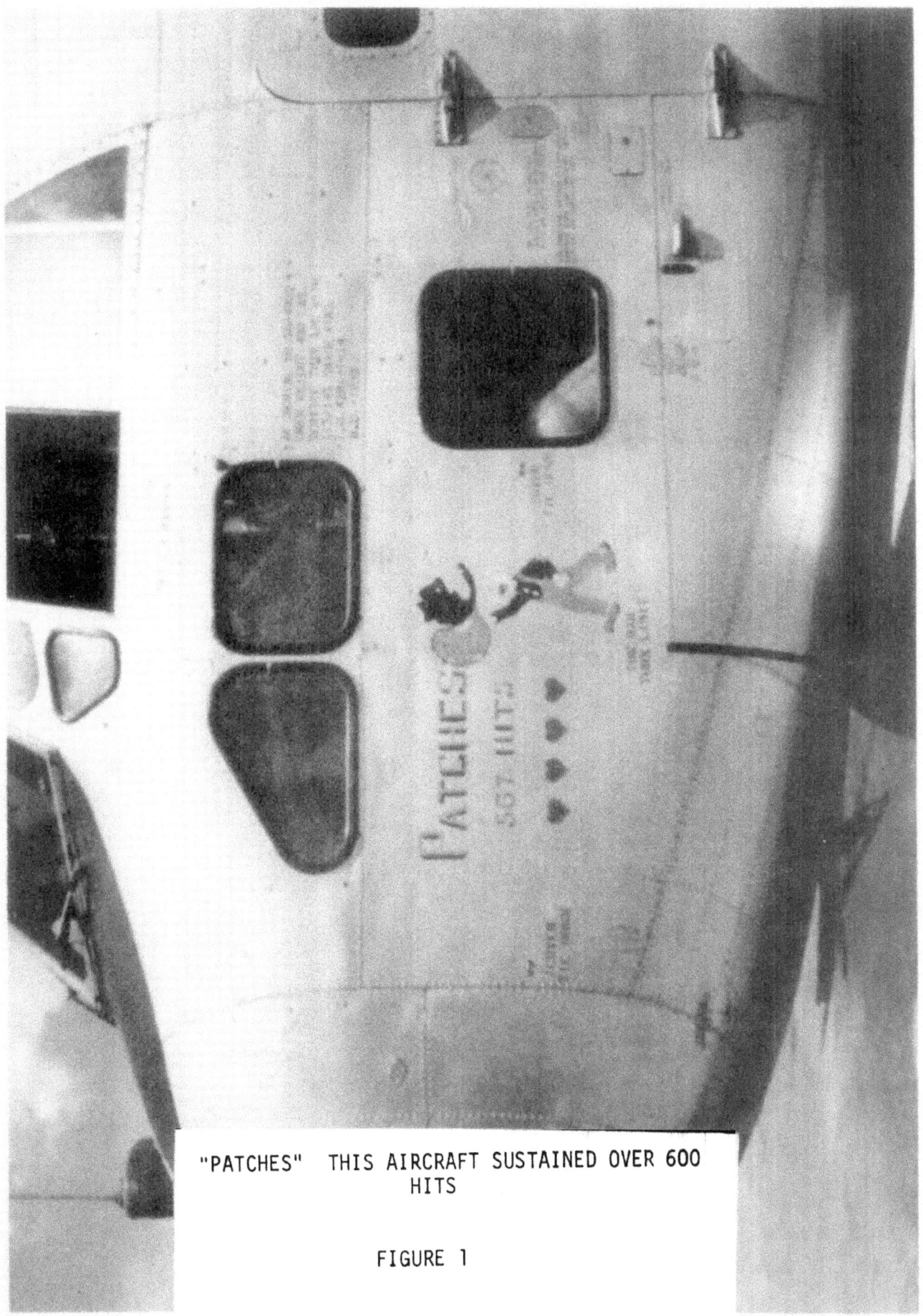

"PATCHES" THIS AIRCRAFT SUSTAINED OVER 600 HITS

FIGURE 1

CHAPTER I

MISSION AND TACTICS

The primary mission of Ranch Hand was defoliation and crop destruction. Defoliation was directed against enemy strongholds, roadsides, powerlines, railroads, and other lines of communication. The objectives were to increase visibility for Forward Air Controller (FAC) and tactical aircraft and to make it more difficult for the enemy to ambush ground forces. Two herbicides were used for defoliation: Orange, a mixture of 2,4-D and 2,4,5-T chlorophenoxy acids (see Chapter IV for a complete description); and White, a mixture of 2,4-D and picloram. Crop destruction was directed at food plots of enemy troops, the objective being to increase their logistics problem. The herbicide used for crop denial missions was Agent Blue, a sodium salt of cacodylic acid.

Proposed targets were carefully screened at all echelons. Requests for defoliation and crop destruction were originated by army commanders at or below the province level. The request, when approved by the Province Chief, was sent to the Vietnamese Joint General Staff (JGS). With their approval, it went to Military Assistance Command, Vietnam (MACV) which reviewed specific target areas and operational requirements. A coordination meeting was then held at the province where the final plan was agreed upon. Following this, an operations order was published by the JGS and an execution order issued by MACV. It required approximately six months from the time the request for defoliation was first submitted until the final plan was agreed upon by all levels of command.[2/]

A second mission of the Ranch was that of conducting airlift operations as directed by higher authority. This was accomplished by removing the spray tanks and spray booms from the aircraft and installing the conveyors and other essential equipment for airlift operations. The conversion, when required, was accomplished in less than 24 hours.

Two airplanes assigned to Ranch Hand operated under control of the MACV Command Surgeon. These aircraft were equipped for spraying malathion only, an insecticide which kills mosquitoes. Fourteen targets consisting of military bases and parts of their adjacent cities in South Vietnam were sprayed at nine-day intervals to achieve maximum effectiveness.[3/]

Ranch Hands flew their early missions with the UC-123B PROVIDER, later equipped with J85-GE-17 jet engines under each wing and redesignated UC-123K. Each aircraft was equipped with a one-thousand gallon tank in the cargo compartment in which the herbicide was carried and dispensed through spray nozzles. Nozzle equipped pipes were located under each wing, and a third boom extended aft through the open cargo door. For optimum effectiveness, Ranch crews flew approximately 100 feet above the terrain or jungle canopy at 130 knots (with installation of the improved A/A 45Y-1 Dispenser System in mid-1966, airspeeds were increased to 140 knots). This provided an effective swath width of 300 feet. In order to insure that the spray would settle where intended, operations were conducted only when the temperature was below 85 degrees Fahrenheit and the wind less

SEVEN-AIRCRAFT DEFOLIATION MISSION

FIGURE 2

than 10 knots. Also, for maximum effectiveness, an absence of precipitation in the sprayed area for two hours after application was essential.

For defoliation, Ranch Hand aircraft were flown on target in three to six-ship echelons making spray runs of approximately four minutes. Occasionally the pilots flew a plumb-tree or race track series on large target areas. The plumb-tree was accomplished by making a 90-270 degree turn at the end of a run to align the formation for a run parallel to, but in the opposite direction from, the first run. The race track was obtained by making multiple runs parallel to each other, beginning at the same end of the target. If any ship in the formation reported ground fire during a run on target, no additional passes were made.

Crop targets were the most dangerous since the planes were on target from five to fifteen minutes, usually in relatively open areas where enemy ground fire was most effective. A three-ship formation was most frequently employed. The flight approached the target in a staggered-V formation and turned the spray on and off as they approached crop boxes. The lead aircraft was responsible for the centerline crop, in addition to directing the wingmen to spray areas on either side of him. The lead aircraft also served as crop spotter and directed the wingmen into proper spray positions. Forward Air Controllers (FACs) accompanied each mission providing an additional source of information on crop location.

When an aircraft took ground fire, the lead ship was notified of the location. A smoke grenade was then thrown by the flight engineer of the aircraft taking fire, and fighters were then released by the FAC, after he had permitted the spray aircraft to reach a safe altitude of 2500 feet above ground level (AGL), to attack the enemy position.

In the early days of herbicide operations heavy suppression was used only when intense ground fire was expected. However, after a Ranch Hand flight took 46 hits on 22 July 1970, heavy suppression tactics were ordered for all crop destruction missions.

For heavy suppression, fighter aircraft preceded the spray planes on target, deploying antipersonnel (CBU) ordnance (CBU 24, CBU 30, CBU 48). These tactics provided a 20-second lead time for the Ranch Hand aircraft. Most suppression missions were flown by F-100 aircraft whose ordnance delivery was accurate and timely. Heavy suppression did, however, have drawbacks. Since CBU 24 ordnance had about a two percent dud rate it was frequently necessary for ground commanders to deny clearance for movement of friendly troops through the area. 4/

Ranch Hand was notified when a new area was being considered for crop denial operations. Ranch personnel conducted their own survey of the target area. Survey flights were made to determine the type of foliage, best herbicide to use, and checkpoints for navigation. In this way, a priority one target could be sprayed approximately five days after it was cleared. The approved area was referred to as a "target box" and the Ranch Hand targeting section was permitted to select areas within the "box" to be sprayed. A mission request was then submitted to Headquarters, 7th Air

RANCH HAND AIRCRAFT OVER PHAN RANG FLYING
IN A WING TIP (DIAMOND) FORMATION

FIGURE 3

Force (Hq 7AF) five to 10 days prior to the spray date and a warning order sent to all agencies five days prior to the mission. However, when weather, maintenance, or supply problems precluded spraying a target on the date requested, a new mission request was submitted. This time delay which resulted from the extensive coordination required for herbicide operations often permitted the enemy to harvest the crop and move on.

CHAPTER II

HERBICIDE OPERATIONS
1961 - 1967

Initial consideration of herbicide operations in the Republic of Vietnam (RVN) came in July 1961 with a Chief, Military Assistance Advisory Group, Vietnam (CHMAAGV) recommendation that chemicals be used to destroy the forest cover along communications routes and to deny the enemy his sources of food. From this suggestion Chemical Division Test Center/ Republic of Vietnam Armed Forces (CDTC/RVNAF) was formed and research initiated on the practicability of crop destruction and defoliation operations. The first field test of this concept was conducted in August 1961, along Route 13 in the district of Chon Thanh, Bien Hoa province. [5/]

The Special Aerial Spray Flight (SASF), Tactical Air Command (TAC), Langley AFB, Virginia, was queried on the capabilities of the C-123 as a spray aircraft for herbicide operations following successful completion of the August 1961 test. Prior to this time, SASF had been engaged in insecticide operations in the United States.

In November 1961, following a favorable response from SASF (TAC), six C-123 aircraft were modified to accept MC-1 spray modules and sent on temporary duty (TDY) to Clark AB, Philippines. They were in place by 6 December 1961. Deployment of three of these aircraft and their crews to Tan Son Nhut Airfield, RVN, was included under Project Farmgate, the first USAF deployment to RVN. They arrived on 7 January 1962 to carry out the specific operations plan published the previous month, code named

"Ranch Hand."[6]

The first Ranch Hand aircraft flew missions from 12 January 1962 through 20 March 1962. These missions were conducted along Route 15 northwest of Saigon and in the Ca Mau Peninsula.[7] These first missions were designed to test the feasibility of large-scale herbicide operations. Testing was completed on 20 March 1962, and further operations were not undertaken pending evaluation of the chemical effects on the foliage.[8]

In April 1962 an Army evaluation team concluded that spray operations "were effective in improving roadside and jungle visibility as an aid in aerial and ground surveillance of routes of enemy movement and supply, to reduce ambush opportunities for the enemy, and to aid in exposing enemy jungle areas." However, the team recommended larger concentrations of the spray be used (up to one and one-half gallons per acre).[9]

Upon completion of this evaluation, the Ambassador and Commander, United States Military Assistance Command, Vietnam (COMUSMACV) were delegated authority to conduct defoliation missions following certain guidelines, e.g., "such operations would not include crop destruction and would be limited to clearing roadsides, powerlines, railroads, and other lines of communication, and the areas adjacent to depots, airfields, and other field installations."[10]

In August 1962 following modification of Ranch Hand aircraft to spray one and one-half gallons per acre, defoliation requests were approved for canals in six areas of the Ca Mau Peninsula. These areas were sprayed and provided additional test data for the period 3 September 1962 to 11 October 1962.[11]

In December 1962 targets were sprayed along roads located in the mountains near the city of Qui Nhon. Following these missions operations were terminated until June 1963, as defoliation chemicals were found to be most effective during the wet season when the vegetation was growing. Therefore, during the period January to May 1963, Ranch Hand aircraft were used for logistical support, navigational aid testing, and radar target missions.[12]

In June and July 1963, defoliation missions were resumed in the Ca Mau Peninsula and along the powerline from Dalat to Saigon. Vietnamese Air Force (VNAF) H-34 helicopters aided in the second operation where mountainous terrain made low-level flying extremely hazardous.

From 31 August 1963 to 16 September 1963, Ranch Hand aircraft were diverted for use in insect control in Thailand. During October-November 1963 the defoliation missions in RVN were resumed.[13]

In September 1963 MACV evaluated herbicide operations in RVN, examining operations between September 1962 to September 1963. This evaluation, requested by the Department of Defense (DOD), concluded that defoliation operations were of definite military value in counterinsurgency operations and recommended that the program be continued.[14]

With the approval of the State and Defense Departments, the program was expanded. In January 1964 authority was delegated to division senior advisors for hand-spray operations. This was particularly useful in reducing the lag time that had existed from proposal to completion of small defoliation projects.[15]

Ranch Hand aircraft were used mainly for Mule Train logistics missions and Tactical Air Positioning System (DECCA) tests from January to June 1964, although some defoliation missions in the Mekong Delta were flown during this time.[16]

Due to heavy concentrations of Viet Cong (VC) in the delta area north and south of Ca Mau, Ranch Hand crews developed the "pop-up" delivery technique. This involved flying very low (20 feet above the ground) through open areas and then "popping-up" to 150 feet for the spray run over the target. However, increased hits from enemy ground fire caused reevaluation of these tactics, and a decision was made to schedule multiple targets. This permitted pilots to break-off from a hot target and spray one that was not so active. As an additional measure, the decision was made that no single target would be sprayed more than two days in succession.[17]

From early July to 22 July 1964, Ranch Hand sprayed many targets in the delta region, defoliating VC safe havens such as the mangrove areas in the Go Cong Province.[18]

It was during May 1964 that the first pilots reported to Ranch Hand on permanent change of station (PCS). During their first two and a half years in Southeast Asia (SEA), Ranch Hand crews had been assigned for a four to six-month TDY tour.[19]

Originally there was a natural aversion to destruction of food resources. However, at the request of the Government of Vietnam (GVN) and following extensive evaluation a decision was made to fly limited crop destruction missions. The first crop denial missions were flown between 21 and 23 November 1962, in Phuoc Long Province, with significant success. Several more crop targets were sprayed between November 1962 and March 1963.

On 20 March 1963 the U.S. Embassy, with MACV concurrence, requested that crop destruction and defoliation missions be continued where their employment would hurt VC military efforts. Also requested was authority for the Ambassador and COMUSMACV to approve crop destruction missions. Crop destruction missions were approved for areas outside of RVN government control by the Assistant Secretary of State for Far Eastern affairs and the Department of Defense (DOD) from March 1963 to July 1964. But delegation of authority for crop destruction missions to the Ambassador and COMUSMACV did not come until 29 July 1964. The total area of foodstuffs sprayed up to that time was 1,325 hectares, (approximately 3,274 acres).[20]

In July 1964 the SASF became Detachment #1 of the 315th Troop Carrier Group operating with the 309th Air Commando Squadron. C-123 Ranch Hand aircraft were modified to include a new pump installation, permitting an increased flow rate of three gallons per acre.[21]

Defoliation operations continued through the fall of 1964. On 3 October 1964 the Ranch Hand crews flew their first crop destruction mission under the Farmgate concept (utilizing mixed VNAF/USAF crews), which involved the major food producing areas adjacent to War Zone D (northeast of Saigon). This project, nicknamed "Big Patches," covered a period of ten days and was highly successful.[22]

During 1964, a total of 257.7 square kilometers of roads, railroads, canals, and VC base areas were defoliated and 15,215 acres of crops were destroyed.[23]

Ranch Hand operations continued to expand in 1965. Project 20-33 originally included 15 individual targets; three additional targets were added later. Targets were heavily foliaged areas along roads and railroad lines. Forty sorties flown during a 14-day period of January 1965 dispensed 36,600 gallons of herbicide.[24] Forty-two additional sorties were flown from 1 March to 19 March 1965, delivering 27,000 gallons of herbicide.[25]

During Project Sherwood Forest, 78,800 gallons of herbicide were delivered between 22 January and 18 February 1965. Sherwood Forest, the first of three jungle burning operations, was a failure. Its failure, however, was not attributable to defoliants.[26]

Following Sherwood Forest, Project Yankee continued with crop destruction in the "enemy rice bowl" of the northern coast, the An Lao Valley, Binh Dinh Province. Operations started on 27 March 1965 and ended on 18 April 1965. Thirty-seven sorties were flown, 27,300 gallons were dispensed, and substantial quantities of foodstuffs were destroyed.[27/]

Project Swamp Fox, the largest defoliation project to that time, was initiated on 30 April 1965. The targets included VC strongholds in the Bac Lieu, Ba Xuyen, and Vinh Binh Provinces. The project was 70 percent complete when it was terminated on 25 May 1965 because of heavy ground fire; however, 77,600 gallons of defoliant were effectively delivered.[28/]

Following Swamp Fox a reevaluation of defoliation operations was conducted by MACV-J2 (Intelligence). The study concluded that defoliation missions were of considerable tactical value, but that operations were to be suspended on 30 June 1965 until additional A-1E crews could complete their training to fly escort for the C-123s. During this interlude Ranch Hand crews flew cargo missions.[29/]

New crop denial missions were flown during the summer and fall of 1965 in Kontum and Binh Dinh Provinces, and on 20 October 1965 operations began in War Zone D. By 17 December 1965, 163 sorties had been flown and 137,650 gallons of chemicals had been dispensed. Fighter support for the spray aircraft included F-100s, F-5s, A-4s, and A-1Es.[30/] Defoliation missions with fire support were resumed in November 1965. They included targets along the banks of the Oriental River where 18 sorties were flown and 14,000 gallons of defoliant were dispensed.[31/] In December, projects were initiated in Kien Hoa and Phuoc Tuy Provinces. In Kien Hoa 70,450 gallons of defoliant were delivered from 7 December 1965 to 31 May 1966.[32/] The Phuoc Tuy project began on 18 December 1965 and ended on 30 January 1966; 60,000 gallons were dispensed.[33/]

Defoliation operations in Laos began in December 1965 under the Tiger Hound program in the Steel Tiger (Panhandle) area of Laos. These activities continued through 31 May 1966, by which time 250 sorties had been flown and most of Routes 92, 922, 96, and 965 had been defoliated.[34/] By 30 June 1966 approximately 1,500 kilometers of roads and trails in Laos had been sprayed to a width of 250 meters on either side. During this time period, 200,000 gallons of herbicides were dispensed.[35/]

Defoliation operations in RVN increased in 1966. During January 130 sorties were flown and 118,500 gallons of chemical were delivered in the Vung Tau, Bac Lieu, Saigon, Nha Trang, and Pleiku areas.[36/] In February 45 defoliation and 48 crop destruction sorties were flown in I Corps and 63 sorties in Laos. The total for February 1966 was 156 sorties which dispensed 145,300 gallons of chemicals.[37/]

A second jungle burning project (the first being Sherwood Forest) was initiated on 24 January 1966. Termed Hot Tip I and Hot Tip II, the objective was the Chu Phong Mountain area, a cluster of peaks and valleys southwest of Pleiku near the Ia Drang River Valley. By 23 February 1966 22,000 gallons of Orange defoliant had been delivered, but the trees would not burn.[38/] The operation was not a complete failure for vertical visibility was substantially improved.

In March, April, and May 1966 more sorties were launched in Kien Hoa and Phuoc Tuy Provinces, as well as in Laos. During March, 116 sorties were flown in RVN and 47 in Laos dispensing 148,450 gallons of herbicide.[39/] In April, the number of sorties flown increased by 20 percent, with a 4.4 percent increase in the amount of herbicide dispensed.[40/] Eleven additional aircraft were programmed for modification and assignment to SASF in May 1966. These were to be delivered by the end of the calendar year. Chemical supplies were also increased to meet the expanded activity. Sorties flown in RVN during May totaled 218, and 199,450 gallons were delivered. In Laos, 23,700 gallons were dispensed in 24 sorties during the same month.[41/]

Major modification of all spray aircraft was undertaken in July 1966. The new spray system was designated the A/A 45Y-1 Dispenser System (some aircraft which were delivered from the United States in 1965 and early 1966 already had the system installed). This new system was capable of spraying 250 to 400 gallons per minute, which was sufficient to provide a coverage of three gallons of defoliant per acre under a variety of tactical conditions.[42/] The completed system had a 20-hp pump which provided the increased spray capability and a 10-inch dump valve which improved the "quick dump" capability from 75 to 29 seconds during aircraft emergencies.

The first documented spray missions flown over North Vietnam occurred in the summer of 1966. Mission coverage ranged from the Mu Gia Pass southward through Laos into the A Shau Valley of South Vietnam.[43/] And by the late fall of 1966, herbicide operations were being conducted in all Corps Tactical Zones of RVN.[44/]

Since November 1965, Ranch Hand had been using seven aircraft. However, in April 1966, COMUSMACV decided to defoliate larger War Zones C and D areas and thus requested 11 additional UC-123s.[45/] Seven new aircraft were received on 10 October 1966, providing SASF with fourteen aircraft at Tan Son Nhut.[46/] Spray operations south of the Demilitarized Zone (DMZ) during the summer of 1966 were operating at a rate of four sorties per day. So many missions were being flown that the supply of herbicide ran low once again, and maintenance began to fall behind. The crews had to slow down to permit supply and maintenance to catch up.[47/]

On 15 October 1966, the SASF of the 309th Air Commando Squadron was discontinued and the 12th Air Commando Squadron (ACS) was formed, retaining the code name "Ranch Hand." The 12th ACS moved to Bien Hoa AB on 1 December 1966 where there was more room for storage and operation.

During December 1966 and January to February 1967, the main areas of activity were in War Zones C and D, as many as 29 sorties were flown daily.[48/]

Project Pink Rose signaled the start of the third jungle burning operation. Pink Rose also included elements of the Strategic Air Command

(SAC) B-52 Arc Light forces from Guam. The target areas (one in War Zone D and two in War Zone C) were selected on 6 November 1966.[49/] Approximately 225 sorties were flown and 255,000 gallons of herbicide were dispensed.[50/] Target areas were ignited from 18 January to 4 April 1967.[51/] However, the technique was ineffective as a means of removing jungle canopy. It was determined that results did not warrant the high cost of resources to continue with jungle burning programs.[52/]

By June 1967, five additional aircraft had been received, raising Ranch Hand's total to 19, all of which were "UC" configured.[53/] From March 1967 to June 1967, Ranch Hand crews participated in many sorties in IV Corps, II Corps, and War Zones C and D. Operations in II Corps included 10 active projects in support of Operations Francis Marion, Pershing, and Byrd, in addition to crop destruction missions.[54/]

After operating in SEA for almost six years (January 1962 to June 1967), Ranch Hand had lost only four aircraft.[55/]

CHAPTER III
HERBICIDE OPERATIONS
1967 - 1971

Although the number of aircraft allocated to the Ranch Hands had increased to 19 by June 1967 (one of which was configured for spraying insecticide only), the increased spray requirements had already outstripped the available planes and herbicide supply. Accordingly, targets were rearranged and priorities adjusted during the early months of 1967. At this time the herbicides Orange and White were made interchangeable because the ultimate effect was the same. [56/]

The 12th ACS continued to expand its operations in 1967. During the first six months Ranch Hands flew 2325 sorties dispensing 1,900,510 gallons of herbicide. [57/]

In September 1967 the 834th Air Division, parent organization of the 12th ACS, completed a study on Ranch Hand resources and accomplishments in order to assess their ability to support increased MACV requirements. The study concluded that the number of planes allocated for spray operations needed to be increased to 32 in order to meet the MACV objectives for the next two years. However, the increase in 12th ACS aircraft assets for spraying did not begin until May 1968.

Weather was a complicating factor in herbicide operations. Optimum effectiveness of the herbicides was achieved only during the peak growing season. And this season coincided with the rainy season, which caused cancellation of missions either because of poor flying weather or heavy rain in the target area which would render the herbicides ineffective. Thus the 834th report was skeptical about the 12th ACS's ability to meet MACV requirements; however, a gradual increase of aircraft assets for the 12th ACS was recommended.[58/]

The 834th Air Division also recommended that the VNAF take over crop destruction missions completely, along with those of mosquito control. However, no action was taken on this recommendation.[59/]

In October 1967 the herbicide program was criticized in a Rand Corporation report. The Rand report was critical of the effectiveness of the crop destruction program:[60/]

> *Data consistently suggests that the crop destruction program has not in any major sense denied food to the VC. Moreover, it appears that it will be exceedingly difficult to accomplish this goal with such a program. The indications are that very negative feelings toward the US/GVN are aroused as a consequence of the spray, and a number of subjects (Vietnamese farmers) speak of increased support for the VC resulting from such operations.*

The conclusion of the Rand report was that crop destruction "may be dysfunctional" and "counterproductive in the long-range US/GVN pacification effort."

The effects of the Rand report were immediate. Headquarters MACV and 7AF pointed out that the program had been requested by the Government of Vietnam (GVN) and that intelligence reports refuted the Rand conclusions.

However, a civilian advisory group from Headquarters, Pacific Command (PACOM) was called in to review and document the effects of crop destruction activities in 1967. The PACOM report, based upon captured documents and an analysis of 622 sorties flown in 1967, disclosed that crop destruction was a vital part of economic warfare. The enemy documents revealed that the VC had suffered serious personnel losses due to the lack of food. Troops normally used in fighting had to be detailed to crop raising, and in one case the 95th North Vietnamese Army (NVA) regiment had to fast for one or two days on several occasions due to a lack of food. The overall conclusion of the PACOM report was that crop destruction was "an integral, essential and effective part of the total effort in South Vietnam."[61/]

Despite these findings, the Chief of Staff, United States Air Force (USAF) requested a thorough study of crop destruction operations in RVN. Hq 7AF initiated the study through Project CHECO at Tan Son Nhut AB, RVN. The CHECO report compiled from captured documents, interviews, and 12th ACS records detailed the crop destruction program and its overall effectiveness. There was evidence that the VC had been forced to reduce the size of their cultivated plots and switch to the "slash-and-burn" technique, attempting to conceal these smaller plots inside tree lines, on mountainsides, and in bombed-out structures. Their tactic was to have one unit move through an area, clear it and move on. A second unit followed to plow and plant, while a third unit was detailed to harvest the crop when ready. However, USAF crews were quite proficient in distinguishing the VC "slash-and-burn" areas from the cultivated Montagnard plots.

A second objective of the crop destruction program was to separate the VC from the people by forcing refugee movements into GVN controlled areas. Intelligence reports documented the success in achieving this objective. In many areas, crop destruction activities not only denied the VC food but also the people contact so essential to the guerrilla-type operations employed by the VC. Captured enemy documents revealed that the crop destruction program was effective. In a letter signed by the Communist Command in III Corps, the VC were informed that their monthly ration of rice for October 1967 was restricted to 25 liters per person due to allied ground operations, bombing, defoliation, and the reducted contributions of the local populace.

A 7AF report on herbicide operations, prepared in 1967, stated that crop destruction forced the enemy to abandon base camps, seek out hidden areas for planting, expend money and personnel to buy and transport food, protect food caches and harass the local population for more food. Also, the report went on to note, that the previously discussed Rand paper was weak in two areas: (1) the period covered did not include the major changes in the crop destruction program made in June of 1967; and (2) the report did not consider the important interrelation of crop destruction and the overall MACV crop denial strategy. The 7AF report documented the value of crop destruction, refuted the Rand report, and justified the continuation of the crop destruction program in 1968 and 1969. However, the restrictions which had governed the program from its inception remained in effect. 62/

From July to December 1967 Ranch Hand crews flew 2856 sorties dispensing 2,676,080 gallons of herbicied. Crop destruction missions accounted for 415 of the sorties. During this time, Ranch Hand aircraft received a total of 296 hits and one aircraft was lost to enemy ground fire. 63/

The TET Offensive began in early 1968. During this offensive herbicide activities were terminated and the aircraft returned to the 315th Air Commando Wing for airlift operations. The UC-123's were deconfigured, that is, spray equipment removed and conveyors and associated airlift equipment installed within 24 hours. The 12th ACS flew 2,866 airlift sorties in support of allied operations. By the time spray activities were resumed, the results of the UC-123 tests at the Air Proving Ground Center, Eglin AFB, Florida, had been reviewed and approved. These tests were designed to measure the performance of the UC-123 when one engine was damaged during a spray mission. When two jet engines were mounted to the wings and other modifications completed the aircraft was redesignated UC-123K. One of the other modifications was the installation of a larger spray pump so that the volume of spray could keep pace with the increased speed at which the plane could now fly. A flow meter was installed to insure even distribution of three gallons per acre regardless of the plane's speed. All 31 aircraft earmarked for Ranch Hand were scheduled for the modification beginning in July 1968.[64]

Throughout 1968 the herbicide program was subjected to searching evaluation. The first comprehensive review was requested by the American Ambassador in January 1968 and culminated in May with the publication of a report. The findings were largely favorable to the program. From the military point of view the herbicide program was considered successful, especially with respect to defoliation. However, the review was less enthusiastic about crop destruction. It recommended limitations on spraying in populated enemy areas, improved psychological warfare operations (psyops) to combat enemy propaganda, and improved indemnification programs to make the use of herbicides more acceptable to the people. The review committee concluded that the ecology of RVN had not been affected by the use of herbicides and that the soil of the country had not been rendered sterile at any time. In August 1968, COMUSMACV sent another report on herbicide operations to the Commander-in-Chief, Pacific (CINCPAC) which concluded, "all field commanders, without exception, state that herbicide operations have been extremely effective in assisting the Allied combat effort."[65] In September yet another military evaluation was directed by COMUSMACV and the results, presented in October, again justified continuation of herbicide operations.[66]

Herbicide missions flown during 1968 were essentially the same as those of previous years. Targets included enemy base camps, roads and trails, canals, and crops. The major difference from previous years was a reduction in the number of sorties flown and acres sprayed. An average of 15.3 aircraft were utilized each month; 5,745 sorties were flown during the entire year. VNAF participation in the program increased in both target selection and mission execution.[67]

By the end of 1968, a shift in emphasis of herbicide operations was evident. As detailed in the 1968 Combined Campaign Plan, herbicide operations were directed at (1) allied lines of communication; (2) enemy routes of supply; (3) base areas which were the object of allied operations; and (4) buffer zones along RVN borders.

The crop destruction program had been highly successful, yet its political ramifications were a constant problem, both in Vietnam and the United States. In 1968, only five percent of all herbicide missions were for crop destruction, and the general pattern for 1969 reflected the same proportion of effort.[68]

Herbicide missions continued through 1969 with crew members flying an average of 430 sorties monthly. Aircraft allocations for spray operations increased to a peak of 33 in October.

The phase-down of herbicide operations in RVN began in November 1969 with the redistribution of 19 spray aircraft to other squadrons within the 834th Air Division.[69]

In January 1970, only 346 sorties were flown in RVN, even though the RVNAF JGS added Phu Bon and Kien Giang Provinces to the spray target areas.[70] Further reductions were forecast when in February the USAF was notified that the U.S. Secretary of Defense had approved only three million dollars of the 27 million dollars requested by MACV for herbicide operations in FY 71. Based on this budget the USAF Chief of Staff advised CINCPACAF that all herbicide stocks would be depleted by 30 November 1970 at the programmed consumption rate. The following alternatives were presented to CINCPACAF:[71]

1. Operations could continue at the programmed rate until herbicide stocks were depleted, after which the 12th SOS would be withdrawn from RVN.

2. Operations could continue at the programmed rate through FY 70, at which time the 12th SOS would be reduced to a minimum level for emergency needs, consistent with the approved budget.

3. Immediately reduce the 12th SOS to eight aircraft and control herbicide expenditure so as to deplete the stock (within the approved budget) at the end of FY 71.

CINCPACAF advised the Commander-in-Chief, Pacific (CINCPAC) who in turn notified COMUSMACV of the budget cuts and the resultant program adjustments.[72] CINCPACAF then responded to the Chief of Staff, USAF, recommending that the 12th SOS be reduced to eight aircraft, and that these be used only for high priority targets.[73] The recommendation was approved and by 30 June 1970 the 12th SOS was reduced to eight aircraft, with two configured for insecticide spraying.[74/] Thus herbicide operations were reduced to 132 sorties per month to spray high priority targets.[75/]

On 6 April 1970, the 12th SOS was directed by Hq 7AF to deploy three aircraft to Da Nang, augmenting the four plane detachment already there for operations scheduled on 10-11 April 1970.[76/] The Bien Hoa aircraft departed on 9 April 1970 to participate in one of the Ranch Hand's most challenging operations. It was a seven-ship spray operation, with four F-100 fighters, six Huey gunships, and ten Cobra Gunships providing armed escort. The targets were enemy crops in the Song Be Valley, Quang Ngai Province. The mission was successful; but the formation took 37 hits from enemy ground fire.[77/] Upon completion of the operation, the three specially deployed aircraft returned to Bien Hoa.

On 21 April 1970 the Da Nang detachment of the 12th SOS, known as "Mountain Ranch," was recalled to Bien Hoa. This detachment was deactivated, its aircraft deconfigured, and transferred to the 315th TAW at Phan Rang AB.[78/]

It was during this time period that laboratory studies in the United States concluded that dioxin, a trace contaminant in Orange, might cause birth defects or abnormalities in human beings; the teratogenic effect. (See Chapter IV and Appendixes for Biological Aspects of Herbicides.) Although response by laboratory animals was not uniform and all species did not evidence effects, a temporary suspension order on the use of Orange was issued in April 1970.[79/]

With the suspension of Orange, Ranch personnel foresaw problems in targeting. There was only a limited number of targets which could be sprayed with Blue. Also all targets previously scheduled for Orange had been switched to White, and the supply was nearly exhausted by early May.[80/] The phase-down of herbicide operations was now apparent to all, with a decrease in sorties flown from 346 in January to 132 to April.[81/]

During the Cambodian incursion the Ranch Hands suspended herbicide operations. On 9 May, the 12th SOS received a message from Hq 7AF conveying the possibility of using Ranch aircraft on psyops missions of leaflet drops as directed by MACV and for night flare drops in support of Cambodian operations.[82/] Upon receipt of the message, the 12th SOS began to reconfigure the spray planes for flare capability. Hq 7AF had expected the conversion to require 17 days; however, Ranch crews accomplished the task in six days.[83/]

On 11 May, the 12th SOS sent aircrew and support personnel TDY to Nakhon Phanom AB, Thailand, to study flare operations with the 606th SOS. Upon their return they participated in several briefings and helped to establish some basic operational procedures for flare missions. Mark-24 flares were to be used in the operations, each having a 2¼ million candle power and an illumination period of three minutes. The Mark-16 white phosphorus marking flares were also used as navigational aids in positioning the Mark-25 flares over the desired area.[84/]

Their first flare mission was flown on 16 May in northeastern Military Region (MR) IV where 27 flares were dropped. The second mission was flown over Cambodia where 96 flares were dropped. Flare operations generally involved the scheduling of three aircraft. Two were launched before midnight and the third was kept on alert with a twenty minute launch capability from midnight to 0600 hours. Operations continued in this manner until 11 June 1970. The squadron received fragmentary orders directing the deployment of one flare aircraft to Pleiku on the afternoon of 11 June to operate there for five days. After five days, another crew arrived from Bien Hoa to replace the earlier one. Operations continued out of Pleiku until 29 June, when the aircraft and crew were directed to return to Bien Hoa. 85/

The primary purpose of flare missions was to support the Cambodian operation. With the withdrawal of U.S. forces from Cambodia by 30 June 1970, Ranch Hand flare missions decreased. The last flare mission was flown on 6 July 1970. 86/

Throughout this period, 12th SOS aircraft flew psyops missions. The Squadron was assigned leaflet drop missions under the direct control of the 9th SOS at Bien Hoa AB. The Ranch Hand crews flew their first psyops mission on 11 May 1970 in MR III. For the next 15 days the squadron was scheduled for two missions daily. On 25 May the psyops requirement was decreased to one mission daily and on 6 July 1970 the last leaflet mission was flown. The majority of the Ranch

Hand psyops missions were flown into Cambodia; however, some were dispersed throughout MRs II, III, and IV of RVN.[87]

On 13 June 1970, a request was made to CINCPACAF for the deactivation of the 12th SOS. Seventh AF authority to relocate the Ranch Hand aircraft at Phan Rang AB was granted on 28 June 1970. The move was completed by 10 July 1970. CINCPACAF approval for deactivation of the 12th SOS was received on 2 July. The 12th SOS was formally deactivated on 31 July 1970, and the Ranch Hand unit assigned to Phan Rang was designated as "A Flight" of the 310th Tactical Airlift Squadron.[88]

On 17 July, COMUSMACV cancelled all fixed wing defoliation missions; however, fixed wing crop denial missions with agents Blue and White were to be continued.[89] Thus with deactivation of the 12th SOS, reduction in the number of aircraft, and cancellation of defoliation missions, the phaseout of Ranch Hand mission continued. However, there were two reservations attached to the deactivation order affecting the 12th SOS: first, the 315th TAW would maintain a defoliation (including crop denial) capability; and second, the Wing would maintain two UC-123 aircraft and crews to continue spraying insecticide in support of the MACV malaria control program.[90]

Herbicide activities designated as crop denial missions were ordered by MACV to begin on 20 July 1970 in MR II and III. However, it had been over two months since the last defoliation mission, and newer crew members were inexperienced in combat. Therefore, training flights were begun on 16 July 1970. The training area was located just north of Nha Trang AB over a "pacified area;" however, when an aircraft was hit on 21 August training was switched to another region. The new training area was over water, and while it provided low altitude flight experience to new crew members it was unrealistic considering the nature of the Ranch mission. Therefore most crop denial missions served two purposes: destruction of enemy crop supplies and training of aircrew members in Ranch Hand techniques.[91/]

Operations from Phan Rang AB produced still more problems for Ranch Hand operations. The storage of herbicides at Phan Rang AB was not permitted by agreement with the local province chief. Storage facilities were located at Da Nang, Phu Cat, and Bien Hoa Air Bases. Thus, missions could be scheduled only every other day, using the day between missions to fly to one of the storage locations to reload the aircraft with herbicide.[92/]

The first crop mission flown by the newly formed "A Flight" of the 310th TAS was on 20 July 1970. The formation sustained 23 hits from enemy ground fire. A second mission on 22 July against a target 20 miles west of Nha Trang AB resulted in 46 hits. As a result of these hits, Hq 7th AF formally designated all crop targets as "high threat" targets, thereby requiring heavy weapons suppression tactics.[93/] From that time on, all herbicide missions were preceded by fighters which dispensed CBU ordnance to suppress enemy ground fire. This tactic was successful: in 11 subsequent missions involving 33 aircraft only 11 hits were sustained.[94/] The requirement for heavy suppression created problems. As previously stated some CBU ordnance had about a two percent dud rate and represented a hazard to friendly ground forces operating in the area. Thus many crop destruction missions were cancelled because clearance was denied by groun commanders or province chiefs. For example, the U.S. 23rd Infantry (American) Division denied clearance for CBU suppression in all of their operational areas. The crop mission could not be flown without clearance for heavy suppression.[95/]

In the summer of 1970, public pressure was building in the United States against herbicide operations in RVN. Politicians and academicians, frequently lacking accurate information on ecological effects, herbicide targets, and military effectiveness of the tactic began publicly to condemn the program. Even within the military community there were mixed views concerning herbicides. Regardless of the validity of these views, the herbicide program in Vietnam was destined to terminate. Various cost analyses showed that the program was uneconomical. Estimates ranged from $29.50 to $52.00 per acre sprayed, yet no one attempted to measure the numbers of lives saved by the military advantages gained from the program, or compare the cost of the herbicide program to other military operations such as Arc Light.[96/]

Crop destruction missions continued through the summer and early fall of 1970, averaging 19 sorties per month, down from the peak of over

430 sorties during 1967-1969. At this point, there was legitimate reason to question the cost-effectiveness of the program. It became increasingly more difficult to justify six herbicide aircraft for only 19 sorties a month. Problems were also encountered in target selection. The Ranch Hand had always relied on MACV for target selection, but made their own occasional survey within approved target boxes to recommend specific areas. In the last three months of herbicide operations, Ranch Hand surveys failed on two occasions to locate any crop within designated target boxes; the entire target area consisted of virgin timber and barren rock plateaus. [97]

In October, COMUSMACV requested that all Orange stocks be consolidated and stored at locations where positive control could be exercised. [98] All attempts at lifting the suspension on Orange had failed, despite scientific evidence demonstrating the fallacy of the "teratogenic effect." [99] COMUSMACV repeated in November 1970 that Orange would not be used and listed the crop destruction targets which had been approved for the following year. [100] However, with the cancellation of further Blue shipments in December the fate of herbicide operations appeared to be sealed. [101] Existing stocks of Blue were insufficient to cover all of the approved targets.

January 1971 brought increased pressure against herbicide operations from many fronts. Heavy pressure from ecologically-minded individuals, high costs of operation, and a continuous lack of clearance into designated target areas were severely limiting factors on continuing the missions. On 3 January, the 834th Air Division requested that Hq 7AF re-evaluate the requirements of the herbicide mission to determine if any of the aircraft could be released for airlift operations.[102/] The 834th received its answer on 9 January: the Air Force crop destruction program was to be phased out by May 1971. Furthermore, crop destruction would be limited to specific projects desginated by 7AF, and no new projects would be forthcoming.[103/]

The last crop destruction mission was flown on 7 January 1971, and on 28 January, JCS officially terminated all USAF crop destruction missions The aircraft and spray systems were to be retained by the 315th TAW until final determination was made on the possible turnover of herbicide capability to the VNAF.[104/] The 315th could deconfigure the spray aircraft as necessary for utilization in airlift operations. However, all spray equipment was to be maintained in ready configuration for possible turnover to the VNAF. The insecticide mission was to be retained.

Thus the herbicide mission of the USAF, code named Ranch Hand, began in January 1962, and was terminated in January 1971. Ranch aircraft received over 4,725 hits from hostile ground fire (Jan 67-Jan 71), according to official records. However, unofficial estimates place the total number in excess of 7,000. The unit was one of the most, if not the most, "shot at" in RVN.

CHAPTER IV

BIOLOGICAL ASPECTS OF HERBICIDES

Herbicides are a group of chemicals used for killing plants or inhibiting their growth. There are two major types of herbicides; the symmetrical triazines and substituted ureas; and the chlorophenoxy acids.

The symmetrical triazines and substituted ureas were not used in RVN defoliation or crop denial operations. Their mode of action is through the Hill Reaction, blocking a critical step in photosynthesis, thus stopping food production and starving the plant to death. 105/

The chlorophenoxy acids are similar to indolacetic acid, a plant auxin (growth hormone). When applied, the plant in essence grows itself to death. These constitute the main bulk of herbicides used in RVN.

Two basic types of defoliants (chlorophenoxy acids) and one crop denial herbicide were used in RVN:

> Agent Orange: A mixture of normal butyl esters of (2,4-dichlorophenoxy)-acetic acid and (2,4,5-trichlorophenoxy)-acetic acid. These chemicals, better known as 2,4-D and 2,4,5-T, respectively are in a 1:1 ratio. Orange is a systemic herbicide effective against broadleaf plants: i.e., jungle growth and mangrove trees. Plants which have been sprayed show a color change in seven to ten days. Maximum effectiveness of the chemical is obtained within four to six weeks after application.
>
> Agent White: A mixture of triisopropanolamine salts of 2,4-D and picloram (4-amino-3,5,6-trichloropicolinic acid) in a 4:1 ratio. White is also a systemic herbicide, similar in action to Orange. Discoloration of

sprayed vegetation appears from ten to fourteen days after application, with six to eight weeks being required for maximum effect.

Agent Blue: A 54 percent solution of cacodylic acid, an organic arsenical with a low mammalian toxicity. Blue is a dessicant, drying out the surface of the contacted vegetation on contact. It produces only temporary effects on broadleaf vegetation but is especially effective against annual narrow leaf plants. Discoloration of sprayed plants occurs within 24 hours, and death follows within two to four days.

Toxicity studies on the active chemicals in each of these agents have well established the fact that they have a very low mammalian effect. The Lethal Dose 50 (LD 50 - dose in milligrams per kilogram of body weight needed to kill 50 percent of the test animals) for the herbicides used in RVN, as compared to aspirin, are given below: 106/

CHEMICAL	LD50
(2,4-dichlorophenoxy)-acetic acid: (2,4-D)	300-1,000
(2,4,5-trichlorophenoxy)-acetic acid: (2,4,5-T)	100-300
Cacodylic acid	830
Picloram	8200
Aspirin	1775

Although these substances have a wide range of phytotoxicities, there is no evidence that they did or could in the future cause toxicity problems for man or other mammals.

EFFECTS OF DEFOLIATION 107/

Climate: It has been said that large-scale modification of vegetation or the denuding of an area will cause a change of climate, particularly in the amount of rainfall. The theory behind this statement holds that as a forest is converted to grassland or the soil is stripped of vegetation the evapo-transpiration surface is reduced, thereby releasing less moisture into the atmosphere, reducing subsequent precipitation. This theory does not consider the large scale of atmospheric air flow with its concomitant moisture and the insignificant reduction in moisture from evapo-transpiration in the areas of defoliation. The relative ratios of one to the other more than offset any detrimental effect with respect to climate.

By applying the reasoning used for an arid area, one may consider some simple calculations for a forest area that is 100 kilometers on a side.[108/] Assuming, conservatively, that the total atmosphere above the area has a depth of 3-km and the air mass is moving over the area at 5-km/hour, the calculated moisture passing over the area is 4.17×10^9 grams per second. Assuming our hypothetical forest has been entirely denuded of vegetation and that it had been contributing 10 percent to the total atmospheric moisture, we can expect a 10 percent decrease of rainfall after the vegetation is removed. Ten percent of the total atmospheric moisture would be 4.17×10^8 grams per second. Thus, our forest would have been contributing moisture to the atmosphere at a rate of 1.1×10^5 gallons per second. Carrying this calculation further, and considering one tree with its branches in the upper or middle canopy for each 10 square meters, the evapo-transpiration from each such area would be 417 milliliters per second. And that is far beyond the measurements that have been made for salt cedar (<u>Tamarix pentandra</u>), one of the heaviest users of water.[109/]

Research by Ohman and Pratt also supports this discussion. They measured dew point over and downwind from a desert irrigation project covering 100,000 acres in Yuma, Arizona (annual precipitation approximately three inches).[110]/ Despite application of annual totals of from five to ten feet of irrigation water on this area extending some 20 miles parallel to prevailing winds for the summer months studied, all influence of the irrigated fields upon crop-level dew points became immeasurably small only 100 feet to the lee of the downwind edge of the entire area. And at 12 feet above the crop level, dew points were not measurably increased, even at points inside the irrigated acreage.

Another point which refutes the evapo-transpiration/precipitation theory is that water molecules are not motionless in the atmosphere. Sutcliffe estimated that the average time between a water molecule's evaporation into and its precipitation from the atmosphere was about 10 days. Thus, from consideration of the mean wind speed, the average water molecule must drift several hundred miles before it is precipitated. There is thus no evidence to support the contention that defoliation in RVN has or will have significant effect on atmospheric moisture or precipitation.

Soils: One of the principal fears of exposing soil in the tropics is the potential for increased laterization. Laterite refers to an indurated concretionary deposit, with high concentrations of aluminum oxide or iron, formed in place by the natural weathering process on rocks. True laterite hardens irreversibly. Laterite has been found to be best developed under the following conditions:

   a. The climate must have high rainfall and uniformly high temperatures.

   b. The topography must have been fairly gentle, peneplain in nature.

   c. A well-drained soil must have been present, frequently alluvial.

   d. There must have been a uniformly fluctuating water table which had a definite low level during the dry season.

   e. Stable geological conditions must have existed for a long time.

About 30 percent of the soils in Vietnam have a potential for laterization. Many of the red soils in Vietnam (often confused with laterite) dry out and become hard, but soften again when wet. The soft doughy laterite, which hardens to a rocklike material when exposed to alternate wetting and drying, is not found in significant amounts in Vietnam.

Two kinds of laterite are found in Vietnam. Wormhole laterite is generally consolidated and occurs as massive beds, commonly at the bottom of a one to 30 foot layer of well-drained soil. It is red to brown in color and has a slaggy appearance due to numerous holes, often interconnecting and thus facilitating the passage of groundwater. Wormhole laterite occurs throughout most of the Mekong Terrace region in soils of both forested and cultivated areas.

Pellet laterite is unconsolidated and occurs as small pellet-like concretions in an iron or aluminum-rich soil. The hard concretions are usually surrounded by fine-grained material that is generally clayey when moist. The coarser particles in this fine-grained material are commonly iron-stained quartz sand. Pellet laterite occurs on the iron-rich basalt plateau soils of the Mekong Terrace, the basalt plateau of Ban Me Thuot, the extreme western edge of the high plateau west of Pleiku, and in a small area around Quang Ngai. Pellet laterite has been observed forming on the metamorphic rocks near Bong Son and on some of the rocks near Qui Nhon. It is likely that wormhole and pellet laterite could occur in the northeastern coastlands, but this has not been evidenced by field studies.

Laterization under natural conditions is a long-term process. The process is accelerated when soil is exposed to direct solar radiation and wind. It is not reasonable to conclude that defoliation in RVN would hasten the laterization process because bare soil does not result from jungle defoliation.

The amount of erosion that occurs as a consequence of defoliation depends on soil type, topography, relative degree of vegetative cover, and the amount and intensity of rainfall. Gully and sheet erosion were in evidence around bases and camps; however, in mountainous and forest terrain no demonstrable effect is found.

<u>Botanical Considerations - Mangrove Forest</u>: The mangrove species are almost uniformly susceptible to White and Orange herbicides, the primary chemicals used in RVN. Rather than being simply defoliated, these species are killed. However, evidence was obtained in 1968 that mangroves defoliated

(and subsequently killed) along the Ong Doc River in 1962 were regenerating. This may be expected to increase more rapidly in that mangrove species produce seeds annually and very prolifically. These seeds have a high rate of germination and remain viable for long periods of time.[111/] The general timetable assumed to be required for the establishment of a dominant, climax mangrove forest is 20 years.[112/] It is therefore logical to expect that the ecological succession of seral stages will take about 20 years, with perhaps a 10-year delay possible, depending on the amount of flooding and pests capable of inhibiting the establishment of a dominant mangrove forest. There is no demonstrable evidence or acceptable theory arguing that the mangrove forests of RVN have been permanently destroyed.

Botanical Considerations - Semideciduous Forests: Trees in the semideciduous forests of Vietnam are also almost uniformly susceptible to defoliation. Data on the regeneration of tropical forests is rare and almost nonexistent for RVN. However, there is no evidence that defoliation has had any effect except to set back the "clock" of ecological succession. Were it not for the presence of bamboo one would expect substantial signs of reforestation. Bamboo, highly resistant to defoliants, moves immediately into those areas which have been defoliated two or more times in a relatively short time, thereby inhibiting growth of the normal deciduous trees. However, on most areas which have only been sprayed with one application of herbicide, the treated area completely recovers within seven years.

Animals: Herbicides are generally considered to have a very low toxicity for man and animals. In order to obtain lethal effects rather large quantities would have to be ingested, as one can see from the table on LD 50s presented earlier. However, there has been considerable discussion of a contaminant (impurity) in 2,4,5-T. The substance is dioxin or (2,3,6,7-trichlorophenoxy)-acetic acid. Preliminary research indicates that dioxin may be as much as one million times more potent as thalidomide in causing birth defects. However, such statements are often misleading. When considering toxicity or mutagenic effects of chemicals on man or animals, one must know whether the effects were obtained with "physiological" or "pharmaceutical" doses. Physiological doses represent the exposure levels expected under normal circumstances, whereas pharmaceutical doses are artificial, synthetic, and meaningless doses, unless the substance being considered is stored by living tissue. It is possible with pharmaceutical doses of common table salt or sugar to produce cancer in laboratory animals, yet under normal usage they are essential for life. The mutagenic effect of dioxin was obtained with pharmaceutical doses, under laboratory conditions. There is no evidence that the small amounts of the substance found in the herbicide 2,4,5-T (also used extensively in the United States), when diluted even further by spraying operations, has ever or will ever produce the mutagenic effect observed under laboratory conditions.

APPENDIX A

BIOLOGICAL/ECOLOGICAL EFFECTS OF HERBICIDES

The material presented in this Appendix was drawn from papers presented by scientists at various technical and professional meetings.

Extracts from the Minutes - Meeting of Defoliants Anti-Crop Systems Subcommittee of the JTCG/CB, 8-9 December 1970, dated 22 January 1971, published by Air Force Armament Laboratory (AFSC), Eglin AFB, Florida. (Extracted information is UNCLASSIFIED, LIMITED OFFICIAL USE.)

INCINERATION OF ORANGE

Combustion experiments have indicated that the safest way to destroy large quantities of Orange is by incineration at a chamber temperature of around 900°C (1652F). At much lower temperatures (100 - 200C), a remote possibility of dioxin formation exists. FDA studies have indicated that the dichlorodioxin from 2,4-D derived phenol was as teratogenic as the tetrachlorodioxin from phenolic decomposition of 2,4,5-T. Mutagenic apprehensions from these dioxins thus rule out any alternative to high-temperature disposal.

Research on incineration of liquid pesticides was conducted by Drs. Fred L. Shuman, Jr., and B. J. Stojanovic at Mississippi State University under USDA Grant No. 12-14-100-9182(34). They reported briefly on "incineration" at the National Working Conference on Pesticide Disposal, held at the National Agricultural Library at Beltsville, Md., on 30 June to 1 July 1970. Additional information on these studies, and others on pesticide disposal, must be obtained directly from the USDA.[113/]

ECOLOGICAL INFORMATION FROM EGLIN AFB

A one-mile square test area at Eglin AFB, Florida, called Range C-52A has been used since 1964 to calibrate and flight test herbicide spray equipment. Since 1964, the following quantities of herbicides have been applied to this one-mile square grid:

```
ORANGE    106,200    gallons
PURPLE     96,600    gallons
BLUE       11,970    gallons
WHITE       8,380    gallons
```

Water and soil samples from this test area were analyzed both chemically and by bioassay techniques. The maximum amount of arsenic found in any of the samples was 3.0 ppm, well below the minimum tolerated for interstate produce traffic. Although different parts of the grid varied in the amount of herbicide residue, the general trend was for the highest concentrations to occur in the first 12 inches of soil. Decreasing residues were found with increasing soil depths.

With the amounts and types of herbicides applied to this grid an area devoid of both vegetation and animal life might be expected. However, this was not the case. There was an adequate ground cover of both grasses and scrub brushes over most of the area. Prior to the establishment of the grid area for agent dispersal studies in 1964, the area was bulldozed and cleared of all vegetation. Along its boundaries were found stands of pine, oak, and other vegetation native to the Florida coastal plain.

During spray missions Eglin AFB monitored the drift to a distance of five miles from the test area, using sensitive indicator plants (potted tomatoes). The plants remained in place for 24 hours after the test missions and were then removed to greenhouses and observed for herbicide effects for 21 days. Only on rare occasions did indicator plants exhibit any herbicide response.

The wildlife on the grid area was kept under continual observation and periodic population counts were made. Animals observed on the grid included deer, fox, wild pigs, turtles, snakes, and mice. Arthropods were also found in abundance and included wasps, bees, ants, and spiders. Population counts showed that more animals were present on the test grid than in neighboring cleared areas. None of the species native to the region exhibited population decreases.

Many small rodents were captured on the grid and examined for congenital defects. None were found. Sixteen pregnant mice captured on the grid were observed to give birth to normal offspring. Three generations of these mice were raised in the Eglin laboratory, with no evidence of congenital defects.

Two small streams crossed the boundary of the grid area. These streams, fed intermittently from the run-off of the grid, were the subject of an ecological study. Adequate vegetation and aquatic life was found to be present in all streams. The principal aquatic plant found was the water hyacinth, and although acutely sensitive to phenoxy herbicides, it was quite abundant.

Investigations were also conducted on the possible accumulation of organic arsenicals (from cacodylic acid - White). Studies considered possible accumulations in both soil and water, as well as oysters, in the Gulf of Mexico at the mouth of the two streams. Oysters seeded in these areas were periodically sampled for arsenic content. The greatest amount of organic arsenical found was 1.0 ppm. Samples from other, nontest areas in Florida indicate that native oysters may contain as much as 42 ppm of organic arsenic.

These studies demonstrated that extensive dispersal of herbicides over the Eglin C52A range did not result in any deleterious effect on wildlife on or adjacent to the test area. The results of plant and soil studies evidenced similar results. No long term effect of herbicide dispersion was demonstrable from an ecological standpoint. [114/]

SUMMATION OF AAAS HERBICIDE ASSESSMENT CONFERENCE, 14-21 JUNE 1970

The 21 specialists attending the conference were asked to consider two central issues: (1) whether significant social, ecological, or economic consequences could derive from use of herbicides in Vietnam and, if so, (2) whether such consequences could be studied.

The following assumptions provided a base for considering the question

> 1. The use of herbicides (defoliants) began in late 1961, peaked in 1967-1969, declined in the first quarter of 1970, and were virtually terminated in April 1970. In the future, they were to be used only on a very limited scale around army camps, on airfields, etc.
>
> 2. During 1962-1969, a total of 5.75 million acres were treated with 17.25 million gallons (product plus diluant) at a product cost of 120.75 million dollars. The application rate was three gallons per acre, the product cost was $7.00 per gallon.

Further, participants were informed that --

> 1. Herbicides had been aerially sprayed on 13 percent of the forest land and seven percent of the crop land during 1962-1969. Calculations for annual treatment on cropland were as follows: 1965 - 1.3 percent; 1966 - 1.7 percent; 1967 - 3.8 percent; 1968 - 1.3 percent.

2. Three types of herbicides were used --

    Agent Orange: 2,4-D and 2,4,5-T used on forests

    Agent White: 2,4-D and Picloram used from 1966, mainly on forests

    Agent Blue: Cacodylic acid used on crops

The meeting began seemingly with enthusiasm for proving that indeed there were dire conséquences related to the use of herbicides in Vietnam, and that soon a case against this military program would be revealed. As the general sessions progressed, however, it became apparent that there simply was not much evidence to support such a position. Even the most ardent previous advocates of "dire consequences" failed to identify areas of significant consequences.

The general sessions consisted of a series of exceptionally good lectures presented by various specialists. Topics mentioned in the lectures that appeared in need of investigation were divided into one of seven subject categories, and participants with special knowledge concerning those subjects were assigned to appropriate working committees. The following represent summaries and pertinent comments concerning these committee reports.

<u>Mangrove Committee</u>: Two unpopulated mangrove areas (Rung Sat and Ca Mau) were treated heavily with herbicides and it was suggested that there might be ecological consequences to this event. That is, shrimp and crabs in mangrove estuaries typically depend on the breakdown of mangrove leaves for food. It was estimated that loss in shrimp and crab

catch could be as high as 5,000 tons. But the statistical method used to arrive at this figure was vulnerable and this estimate was not included in the committee's final report. The committee did not indicate that there were any other consequences from the use of herbicide in the mangrove areas, although it was suggested that such areas like America's redwood forests ought not to be tampered with.

The committee did not present any dramatic consequence from the use of herbicide in the mangrove areas. As it stood, these mangrove areas provided only a supply of wood to producers of charcoal, and a near impenetrable refuge to the Viet Cong. Destruction of these mangrove stands--especially those in the back areas, away from overly brackish water--not only provided easily workable deadwood for charcoal, but in some cases made the land arable for cash crops. Nearer the sea, viable seeds readily took root and the mangroves again began their march back toward the tidal waters.

Succession Committee: The most extensive use of herbicides was in the forest areas. An estimated 13 percent of the forest were treated at least once. But it appeared obvious during the work sessions that any investigator now flying over areas that had been sprayed once during 1962-1969 would be hard pressed to note any damage. These trees did not die, and for the most part had refoliated. Further, tests had been made in Thailand prior to the use of herbicides in Vietnam, and it is now believed to be virtually impossible to identify in Thailand on the ground or from the air any damage to these test areas. There was no development of savannahs or noticeable soil **laterization**. Succession was not a problem.

Frequent treatment with herbicides will kill trees, however, and commercial foresters find this advantageous to harvesting trees. The mangrove kill was undoubtedly high, but most of the tree types were not commercially exploitable, and succession should proceed normally.

Nutrient Budget Committee. This committee determined that if defoliation had resulted in widespread denudation for a three or four year period, then considerable nutrient damping could be expected. But the forests were not totally denuded on a large scale and whatever damage occurred did not persist for even one-half the time suggested. There was very little nutrient damping, if at all measurable.

Toxicity Committee. It appeared unlikely that herbicides used at stated concentrations in Vietnam would have any effect on livestock. Crops destroyed prior to maturity, of course, would not enter food chains. Vegetables that were treated would react almost immediately (pronounced wilting) and would not appear appetizing to consumers. Crops and fruit treated at the moment of maturity and then harvested and consumed immediately would retain traces of herbicide. It was not known whether this would be eliminated when milling husk from rice or removing the peel from oranges and bananas, etc.

The chemicals in herbicides that portend danger are:

> Dioxin: Found in 2,4,5-T, it has a half-life of five hours in sunlight and might have teratogenic effect during the first three months of a pregnancy if the dosage were concentrated, which is unlikely. It was not known whether this would abort foetal development or cause deformity. In the United States mice reacted positively in such tests; however, rats did not.
>
> Arsenic: The committee did not know the amount of arsenics contained in herbicides but suspected that concentration would have to be extremely high (dose per individual per sprayed area) to produce a recognizable effect. An examination of hair and fingernails of those in spray areas was recommended.

The committee was cautioned by Dr. Constable, M.D., about the difficulty of objectively designating herbicides as a direct or single cause of abortion or teratogenic effect. An interview form might reveal that "X" number of females aborted while in refugee status. The actual cause might well have been a physiological or psychological response to the total stress associated with being a refugee; that is, female refugees tend not to menstruate and this might lead individuals to believe they were pregnant. Since no foetus later developed, there would be a tendency for them to conclude that their suspected pregnancy was aborted and that a possible cause was the presence of herbicides in a given area.

Crop Destruction Committee: Although the committee concluded that this area of concern should have low priority in the ranking of problems that could be effectively studied, the committee did submit a calculation showing maximum possible damage that might have resulted from direct application of herbicides on rice land. This calculation assumed that rice was the only crop treated and that the total supply of available specific herbicide was fully utilized and was 100 percent effective where used. The conclusion from this calculation was that 250,000 people were denied rice each year for five consecutive years.

However, the assumptions leading to this figure were not substantiated. Recalculation based on the following provides a more realistic value:

> 1. National rice paddy yields for domestic (traditional) varieties of rice in Vietnam during the period of time studied typically ranged from 1.7 to 2.1 metric ton (MT) of paddy per hectare.
>
> 2. In the particular area treated by herbicides (as identified during the conference), paddy yields probably ranged from 0.8 to 1.0 MT per hectare. This was due to use of relatively inferior seed, relatively low soil nutrient content, low degree of management and water control, absence of fertilizer applications, the generally inferior response in SEA to cultivation of rice on interior cultivated upland rice lands.

Production Assumption:

```
Each      10,000 hectares yields
        x      1 MT of paddy per hectare
          10,000 MT of paddy harvested
        x     65% milling rate to convert paddy to rice
           6,500 MT of rice per hectare
       6,500,000 kg of rice per hectare
```

Consumption Assumption:

Classified documents based on VC POW interrogations reveal that daily VC rice rations range from 500 - 750 grams milled rice per day. Assuming that 600 grams is typical of "average" rice rations, each adult

VC soldier consumes 219 kg milled rice per year, as compared to 192 to 195 kg/year available 1966-1969 for the total population.

Thus 6,500,000 divided by 219 = 29,680 adults were denied a rice supply for each 10,000 hectares of rice totally destroyed in the areas treated with herbicides.

Area Treated Annually and Probable Effect: (Assume all land treated was planted to rice and herbicides were 100 percent effective)

	Area (10,000 ha.) a/	x	29,680 b/
1961	0		0
1962	0		0
1963	0		0
1964	0		0
1965	3		87,672
1966	4		116,896
1967	9		263,016
1968	3		87,672
1969	2		58,448
Total	21		613,704 divided by 5 = 122,740 people per year denied rice

The committee's calculation indicated that the volume of rice destroyed by the crop destruction program amounted to enough rice to feed 250,000 adults each year during 1965-1969; however, recalculation indicated that

a/ Defoliation began in 1961, but purposeful crop destruction began in 1965

b/ Total number consumers affected at typical adult VC consumption rate this could have been true in only one year 1967; and that rice denial was significantly lower than 1/2 that rate in the other four years.

<u>Agricultural Economics and Production Committee</u>. The most important point established by this committee was the fact that the military program for herbicides was never aimed at rubber trees, and that inadvertent drift of herbicides directed elsewhere that did contact rubber trees would not do permanent damage. The 50 percent decrease in rubber production was due to causes other than herbicides.

The herbicide program in Vietnam did not cause significant harm to Vietnam's agricultural production or economy. The forest areas were the most seriously damaged sector, but the damage did not appear to be permanent. The forest ecosystem was not drastically upset, and the forestry industry was not hurt because of herbicides.[115]

Extract from "Toxicity of Herbicides in
Use in Vietnam," Dr. C. E. Minarik, Director,
Plant Science Laboratory, Dr. R. A. Darrow,
Chief, Plant Physiology Division, Depart-
ment of the Army, Fort Dettrick, Maryland,
April 1968.

TOXICITY OF HERBICIDES IN USE IN VIETNAM

ORANGE:

Herbicide Orange, the principal defoliant used in RVN, is composed of the butyl esters of 2,4-D and 2,4,5-T, two of the most widely used herbicides in agricultural and industrial vegetation control. Until 1965, there had been no substantial cause of death to man or animals due to these two herbicides in the more than 20 years that they had been in large-scale use.

In 1965 Di Palma* reported that a man committed suicide by consuming about 6.5 grams of 2,4-D. Millions of gallons of Orange have been handled by ARVN and U.S. personnel during the past five years without any reports of illness even though ARVN personnel frequently work in clothing soaked with herbicide. Personnel involved in manufacturing these herbicides have also been singularly free from ill effects attributable to these herbicides, even though they were exposed to them for long periods of time on a daily basis. It must therefore be concluded that even prolonged exposure to Orange is not harmful to humans except in those rare instances where an individual may have a specific allergy to this substance.

A detailed review of herbicide toxicological data is contained in "Assessment of Ecological Effects of Extensive or Repeated Use of Herbicides" prepared by Midwest Research Institute in 1967. The authors concluded

---

*Di Palma, J. R. (Ed), p. 1003 from Drill's Pharmacology in Medicine, McGraw-Hill Book Co., New York (1965)

that the risk of human and animal toxicity from the use of 2,4-D and its various esters and salts is very, very low. Its possible effects on fish and or fish foods may be a problem under certain conditions." With respect to 2,4,5-T they state, "In summary, 2,4,5-T resembles 2,4-D in its toxicity to animals and fish, but is a little more toxic....no synergistic toxicities were noted in animals as a result of using these mixtures."

The toxicity to fish varies with the species, the salt or ester of 2,4-D or 2,4,5-T employed, and the duration of exposure. For example, the LD_{50} in 48 hours for the dimethylamine salt of 2,4-D for bluegill sunfish is 166-458 ppm, while in 96 hours for fathead minnow it is 10 ppm.

A 2,4-D alkanolamine salt has an LD_{50} of 435-840 ppm for bluegills while the propylene glycolbutyl ether, butoxyethyl, ethyl, butyl, and isopropyl esters have LD_{50}'s ranging from 1.1 to 2.0 ppm.

One ppm is the equivalent of 2.72 pounds of herbicide per acre-foot of water. If three gallons of Orange were sprayed on an acre of water one foot deep, the concentration would be approximately 11 ppm. This would be a toxic dose for bluegills if the exposure to this concentration were 48 hours or longer. In bodies of water deeper than one foot, the concentration would be proportionately decreased. If the herbicide fell on a stream with even a slow current, the herbicide would move down stream and might not expose the fish to the lethal dose for more than a few hours. It should be noted that in the past few years with the large volumes of herbicides being disseminated in Vietnam there have been no reports of fish kill attributed to herbicides.

BLUE:

The active ingredient of Blue or Phytar 560G is cacodylic acid as its sodium salt. Cacodylic acid is dimethyl arsenic acid in which the arsenic is in the innocuous pentavalent state rather than the toxic trivalent state. Cacodylic acid has been used medicinally for years, being administered either orally as pills or by hypodermic injection in doses varying from 0.025 to 0.15 grams per day. Human toxicity information is not available, but personnel involved in the manufacture of this material and who have been exposed to this herbicide over long periods of time feel that the toxicity must be relatively low.

Acute oral toxicity (LD_{50}) of cacodylic acid in rats is 1400 mg/kg for males and 1280 mg/kg for females. Skin tests on albino rabbits with cacodylic acid itself and a commercial formulation of cacodylic acid were found to be essentially nonirritating to the skin. Cows fed 24.5 mg/kg of cacodylic acid daily in a 60-day feeding test showed no arsenic in the milk, but arsenic was excreted, principally in the urine. After 30 days the amount ingested was balanced by the amount excreted. The cows were sacrificed after 60 days and ten tissue components and bone were analyzed for arsenic. No tissues stored arsenic compounds on a cumulative basis even though fractional parts per million of arsenic were detected in the liver, spleen, and pancreas.

Fish were able to withstand concentrations of cacodylic acid of at least 100 ppm for 72 hours. The LD_{50} for Gambosia and Notrophis was reported to be about 631 ppm for 72 hours.

Pink shrimp, eastern oysters, and longnose killifish were able to tolerate 40 ppm for 48 hours with no effects.

A review of data on the relationship between arsenicals and cancer has shown no greater incidence of systemic cancer in humans for those individuals who were exposed to arsenic trioxide over long periods of time than for those who were not. However, there is one report that indicates that cacodylic acid, when <u>injected</u> into mice, produced "profound disturbances of cell division" and stimulated mitosis in cells of the crypts of Lieberkuehn and of transplanted tumors.

Exposure of tadpoles to 100 ppm of cacodylic acid (equivalent to 270 pounds per acre foot of water) produced abnormalities during embryonic development.

Since cacodylic acid is currently being employed at a rate no higher than 9.3 pounds per acre, it is safe to assume that there will be no harm to man or animals at these use rates. The high tolerance of rats, other laboratory animals, and fish to this herbicide place it in a safer category than herbicide Orange.

WHITE:

TORDON 101 mixture which is composed of 2,4-D and picloram as the tri-isopropanalamine salt is the most frequently introduced herbicide in Vietnam.

The toxicity of 2,4-D has been discussed under Orange and will not be repeated. However, since White includes surfactants and other adjuvants, toxicological data on the actual agent has been determined as well as on picloram alone.

Picloram has an oral LD_{50} for rats of 8200 mg/kg; for mice 2000; guinea pig 3000; rabbit 1670 - 2000; sheep greater than 650; and cattle greater than 488.

For TORDON 101, oral LD_{50} for rat has been reported as 3080 mg/kg; for sheep 2000; for cattle greater than 3163.

In a feeding test with a cow, 97.7 of the administered picloram was recovered unchanged in the urine. No picloram was detected in the milk.

The median tolerance limits of TORDON 101 to fish are as follows: fathead minnow - 64 ppm; brook trout - 240 ppm; brown trout - 230 ppm; rainbow trout - 150 ppm; green sunfish - 150 ppm.

Thus, it is apparent that neither picloram nor White is to be considered toxic or hazardous to humans, animals, or fish at the use rates being employed in Vietnam.[116/]

Extract from "Persistence of Herbicides in Soil and Water" by Dr. C. E. Minarik, Director, Plant Sciences Laboratory, Dr. R. A. Darrow, Chief, Plant Physiology Division, Department of the Army, Fort Dettrick, Maryland, April 1968.

PERSISTENCE OF HERBICIDES IN SOIL AND WATER

The persistence in soils and water of the three principal herbicides, Orange, White, and Blue, used in RVN defoliation operations has been evaluated.

2,4-D and 2,4,5-T butyl esters in agent Orange are not persistent in soil. Microbial decomposition takes place rapidly and the chemicals disappear in one to three months at the rates of application used in RVN. Germination tests of Black Valentine beans in soils from areas in Bien Hoa and Binh Long Provinces which had been defoliated with Orange in 1966 showed no residual effects of the chemical.

Agent White, containing a mixture of picloram and 2,4-D amines, shows greater persistence than Orange due to its lower rate of microbial degradation. In Puerto Rico tests, the amount of chemical remaining six to 12 months after direct application to the soil of picloram in amounts four to six times greater than that used in RVN defoliation operations was insufficient to cause injury to planted crop seedlings of all but the most sensitive crop, soybeans. As confirmed in bean seedling tests on soils from two RVN provinces taken from 1966 and 1967 defoliation targets, no persistence of herbicides was found 11 to 17 months after single and double applications of White. It was concluded that despite the greater persistence of White than Orange in soils, the residual amounts are not detrimental to crop growth in sprayed areas in the crop season following defoliation.

Agent Blue or cacodylic acid is rapidly absorbed and inactivated in soils. Field tests have shown that susceptible crops can be planted directly in soils within a few days after application of cacodylic acid at rates greater than the three gallons per acre used in single treatments in RVN.

No direct evidence was found of persistence of toxic residues in surface drainage and streamflow following applications of defoliants in RVN. Streamflow analysis in Oregon and other U.S. locations has shown a rapid dissipation of 2,4-D and 2,4,5-T in drainage waters from aerial spray applications on forested areas. No detrimental effects on fish and other aquatic organisms were noted in streams on sprayed areas. Applications of 2,4-D and related herbicides are made directly into streams and reservoirs for aquatic weed control in temperate climates at rates considerably higher than those used for defoliation in RVN, without detrimental effects on fish and other aquatic organisms or impairment of water quality.

In view of the minimal quantities of herbicide available for surface runoff into watershed drainages and stream flows from defoliated areas due to removal by vegetational interception, soil absorption, and the rapid chemical and photochemical decomposition and microbial degradation in soils, it appears extremely unlikely that toxic amounts of chemical will occur in drainage waters from defoliated areas.[117/]

Paper presented in a Panel Session, American Association for the Advancement of Science, 29 December 1970, Subject: Implications of Continued Military Use of Herbicides in SEA, comments by Dr. Fred H. Tschirley, Agricultural Research Service, U.S. Department of Agriculture.

2,4,5-T, AND DIOXIN

The problem with the contaminant in 2,4,5,-T, insofar as general public knowledge is concerned, arose on October 29, 1969 when a press release from the office of Science and Technology informed the public that 2,4,5-T that was used in a study by Bionetics Laboratories resulted in fetal abnormalities in experimental test animals. Very shortly thereafter a question was raised as to whether this result was a consequence of the 2,4,5-T itself or whether it was a consequence of a contaminant which was known to occur in 2,4,5-T. A subsequent analysis of the sample that was used by the Bionetics Research Laboratories revealed that it did, indeed, contain this toxic contaminant at a level of 27 ± 8 ppm. The specific contaminant of which I speak is the 2,3,7,8-tetrachloro-dibenzo-para-dioxin, commonly referred to as dioxin.

You must understand that there is a family of these chlorinated dioxin compounds, but it is the tetrachloro substitution which is the most toxic and is believed to have the most severe adverse effects.

After it was learned that the sample used by Bionetics did contain a high level of the tetrachloro dioxin, representative scientists of the Dow Chemical Company and of the Food and Drug Administration met together to establish some protocols for further testing with 2,4,5-T to try and establish whether or not it was the 2,4,5-T itself or the dioxin which had actually caused these fetal abnormalities. Essentially, without going into a great detail, it was found that a production grade 2,4,5-T in the Dow studies at rates ranging up to 24 mg/kg were not teratogenic in rats. The Dow Chemical Company also tested the tetrachloro dioxin on rats and found there was no effect at a level of 0.03 mg/kg but some effects did become apparent at a level of .125 mg/kg. So from their studies it was established that the dioxin was, indeed, a teratogen and a potent teratogen, but that the production grade 2,4,5-T was not teratogenic in rats at least in rates up to 24 mg/kg.

The National Institute of Environmental Health Sciences also conducted studies and in their studies on rats they came to essentially the same conclusion as Dow did from their studies, but in further studies on mice the NIEHS studies showed that at rates of 100 mg/kg the production grade 2,4,5-T did result in terata. I should say at this point that the NIEHS studies on mice were all conducted by subcutaneour injection of the 2,4,5-T and the carrier was dimethylsulfoxide.

It's of interest, too, that there are a couple of reports in the literature which demonstrate that DMSO, dimethylsulfoxide, can itself be a teratogen, although admittedly at higher rates than were used when the DMSO was used as a carrier in the NIEHS studies. So this led up to the situation in which studies had shown that terata were not caused in rats but were caused in high dosages in mice. Additional research of course must be completed.

This report will now relate to some of the specific work that the Department of Agriculture has conducted to shed more light on this total dioxin problem, work which this author has participated in. First of all, tetrachloro dioxin is an extremely toxic compound. The LD50 on guinea pigs, which so far as is known is the most susceptible test animal, is .0006 mg/Kilo, so it is an extremely toxic material. One of the things that the Department wanted to know soon was the relative level of this dioxin in various classes of pesticidal compounds. So together with FDA it decided on a list of 18 different compounds which should be analyzed to determine their dioxin content.

On the basis of this survey with the phenoxy materials, out of a total of 79 compounds 53 of them had less than .10 ppm of the tetrachloro dioxin; five out of 79 were in the range from .1 to 1 part per million; nine were in the range of 1-10 parts per million, and 12 were in the range of more than 10 parts per million. The Department also tested a number of chlorophenols and found that there the tetrachloro dioxin occurred in 14 of those compounds but always at a rate lower than .10 ppm; .1 ppm there was the limit of detection.

In other materials which were suspected to contain the dioxin as a contaminant, none was found. So the Department, in capsule summary, did find the dioxin in phenoxy compounds. Researchers were not sure whether they found it in chlorophenols or not because they were at the limit of detection, but if the dioxin was there it was less than .1 ppm. It should be mentioned at this point that despite the fact that 12 of the 79 samples contained greater than 10 ppm of the dioxin, these samples belonged to one chemical company which has since gone out of production of 2,3,5-T, and information to date suggests that the 2,4,5-T that is now on the market contains one-half or less parts per million of the dioxin.

The Department was also immediately interested in how persistent this compound was in the environment. Naturally not enough time had elapsed so that it could get a clear handle on this but as soon as researchers were fortunate enough to have Dow Chemical Company supply them with labelled material they did institute some studies on the persistence of this material in soils. They now have 160 days data, and these data suggest that at the end of 160 days they can account for about 95 percent of the dioxin that was put into the soils. Two different soils were used, one a Lakeland sand which has a very low microbiological activity, the other one a Hagerstown silty loam which has quite a high microbiological activity. In both cases, however, the researchers could recover about 95 percent of the material that had been originally applied. So it would appear at this point that in the soil the tetrachloro dioxin is quite a stable compound.

The Department was further concerned about whether or not plants will absorb the tetrachloro dioxin from the soils, and if so, at what concentrations. Researchers used soybeans and oats as test plants in laboratory studies and found that of the amount that was present in the soil, a maximum of .16 percent was picked up by the plants. The maximum concentration in those plants peaked at 10-15 days and declined thereafter. They don't know the reason for this decline--whether the dioxin moved to the surface and was volatilized or whether it was metabolized--but it is a question that they are working on.

It is important to emphasize that in these plant-uptake studies it was necessary to apply a very high level of dioxin. By calculating on the basis of the uptake of other similar organic compounds and the specific activity of the radioactive materials that were at hand, researchers had to apply 40,000 times as much of the tetrachloro dioxin as the soil would receive by a normal agricultural application, in this case an application of about two pounds per acre. So they had to apply extremely high quantities simply in order to be able to detect this material in the plants.

It is interesting that even though it was possible to detect the small amount of material in the foliage portions of the plants - plants which were carried through to maturity - in no case were researchers able to detect the dioxin in the seed, either in the bean of the soybean nor in the grain of the oats.

Moreover, Department researchers were interested in whether or not the compound tetrachloro dioxin could be photodegraded. In laboratory studies under a lamp with an emission of 310 nanometers they found that the half-life of the tetrachloro dioxin was about 3 1/2 hours. This was in a methanol solution. Thus it is photodegraded quite rapidly under those situations.

They also put some of the tetrachloro dioxin into methanol, sealed it in ampoules, and exposed it to sunlight. Here again the photodegradation occurred quite rapidly.

They do not have real good information on just what the situation is in water. It is reasonably certain that the photodegradation in water is not as rapid as it is when in methanol solution so they are still in the process of attempting to determine in a fairly precise manner at least how quickly one might expect photodegradation to account for or to degrade some of the material that would be introduced into the environment under natural circumstances.

In the laboratory studies it has been shown that the tetrachloro dioxin is degraded to the trichloro. This has been proven by mass spectrometry studies, and it is assumed that there is further dechlorinization down to the di - and the monodiozins. It is only the trichloro dioxin which has been definitely established at this point.

Researchers were also interested in the movement of the tetrachloro dioxin in the soil. Again in laboratory studies using three different soils they were able to establish that the compound is essentially immobile. This was true even in a soil such as Lakeland sand which is about 95 percent sand. The find is quite surprising and this author is not sure whether he is completely ready to believe this as yet because one would think that simply by mass flow of a large amount of water some of the dioxin would carry with it. However, the laboratory studies don't suggest this. But it is indicative that certainly in your heavier soils the movement of this compound is going to be restricted to the surface layer of soils. This is important because if it is restricted to the surface layers of soil then it will be less readily picked up by plants. On the other hand, of course, it is the surface soil which is subject to erosion and thereby this material might be moving into the water courses.

Based on the work that the Department has done, this writer does not feel at this time that the possibility of ingestion of an adequate amount of dioxin to cause damage is a very real possibility, and I say this for a number of reasons. One of these is that the current production of 2,4,5-T, insofar as it is known contains one-half or less ppm of the tetrachloro dioxin. Experts know that photodegradation occurs; it is faster in methanol than it is in water, but this could very well account for some degradation in the environment. They know that plants will pick up the material, but only a very small amount of it; less than .2 of 1 percent of the tetrachloro dioxin present in soil was absorbed by plants, and it did not accumulate in the plants. It built up to a peak and then that peak fell off. Again, they don't know just exactly at this point what happened to it--whether it volatilized or whether it was metabolized. It's extremely important, to know that the dioxin did not occur in the seeds of the crops that were grown to maturity.

Lastly, I base the conclusion that the possibility of hazard from the dioxin is a remote one on the fact that terata have occurred in test animals only when those test animals were subject to massive doses. There is a remaining question that must be answered, and that is the possibility of the accumulation of the dioxin in fatty tissues. Its chemistry would suggest that this is something that could happen. <u>On the other hand, there is no proof either one way or the other.</u> The evidence at hand now is entirely circumstantial, secondary; one can argue either way. The pure and simple fact of the matter is that at this point experts don't know and so they have to find out. If tetrachloro dioxin does accumulate in fatty tissues, there are, of course, problems. If it does not, then the possibility of hazard is all the more remote.[118]

APPENDIX B

RANCH HAND SORTIES (HERBICIDE, INSECTICIDE, LEAFLET)

GALLONS OF HERBICIDE DISPENSED

AIRCRAFT ASSIGNED TO RANCH HAND

119/
1967

UC-123 Sorties	July	August	September	October	November	December
Herbicide	536	480	441	548	618	571
Insecticide	20	23	17	21	16	21
Herbicide Dispensed (Thousands gallons)	435.8	343.	400.7	455.7	532.9	503.2
Aircraft Assigned	19	19	19	19	19	19

1968[120/]

UC-123 Sorties	Jan	Feb	Mar	Apr	May	Jun	Jul	Aug	Sep	Oct	Nov	Dec
Herbicide	580	69	284	619	672	613	558	500	398	348	435	669
Insecticide	27	22	25	25	19	19	14	28	21	24	28	28
Herbicide Dispensed (thousands gallons)	550.7	50.2	220.0	560.5	575.1	484.9	411.8	367.1	272.8	289.1	306.7	550.8
Aircraft Assigned	19	19	19	19	21	21	21	21	21	21	21	25

1969 121/

UC-123 Sorties	Jan	Feb	Mar	Apr	May	Jun	Jul	Aug	Sep	Oct	Nov	Dec
Herbicide	514	377	594	449	497	481	424	433	287	441	375	322
Insecticide	10	21	27	38	48	49	45	44	35	39	20	14
Herbicide Dispensed (thousands gallons)	404.9	293.0	539.7	386.9	409.3	401.9	297.2	327.1	230.8	379.3	313.1	282.6
Aircraft Assigned	25	22	22	22	27	29	29	29	27	33*⟶*14	14

*Redistribution of aircraft to other squadrons.

122/
1970

UC-123 Sorties	Jan	Feb	Mar	Apr	May	Jun	Jul	Aug	Sep	Oct	Nov	Dec
Herbicide	346	218	208	132	39	0	18	21	21	19	18	6
Insecticide	33	24	33	27	40	46	50	49	52	45	47	40
Leaflet	0	0	0	0	34	32	3	0	0	0	0	0
Herbicide Dispenses (thousands gallons)	298.6	171.7	152.3	112.3	37.6	0	13.3	18.9	12.8	16.2	11.3	10.6
Aircraft Assigned	14	14	14	12	11	8	8	8	8	8	8	8

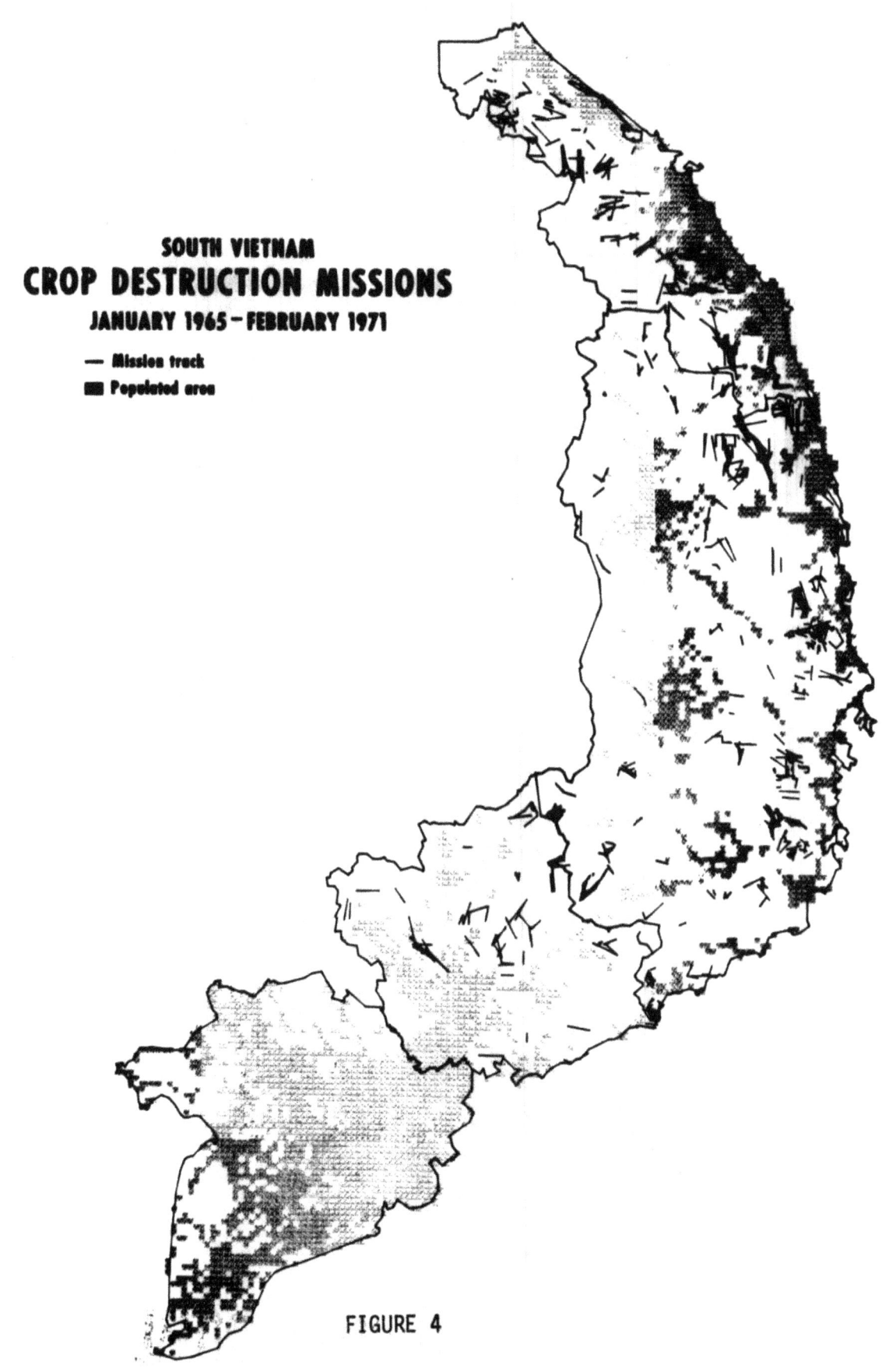

FIGURE 4

FIGURE 5

FIGURE 6

1971 [123/]

UC-123 Sorties	Jan	Feb	Mar
Herbicide	3	0	0
Insecticide	40	33	42
Leaflet	0	0	0
Herbicide Dispensed (thousands gallons)	1.9	0	0
Aircraft Assigned	8	*2	*2

*Retained for insecticide operations.

APPENDIX C

HERBICIDE PROJECTS ALL CORPS

1967 - 1971

This Appendix was compiled from MACV/J3 Surface Operations Division, "Herbicide Operations Report," dated May 1971.

Areas sprayed should not be construed as representing total sprayed area in RVN, as many targets were covered more than once.

PROVINCE	PROJECT NUMBER	GALLONS	ACRES SPRAYED	MISSION TYPE
Quang Nam	10766	7010	2073	Defoliation
Quang Nam	13366	7920	2344	Crop Destruction
Quang Nam	10666	2000	592	Crop Destruction
Quang Ngai	10167	4150	1229	Defoliation
Quang Ngai	13466	7190	2126	Crop Destruction
Quang Ngai	10266	22315	6604	Crop Destruction
Quang Ngai	10167	44990	13324	Crop Destruction
Quang Tin	12166	4655	1377	Crop Destruction
Quang Tin	10266	12590	3726	Crop Destruction
Quang Tin	16766	2770	820	Crop Destruction
Quang Tin	10766	30210	8920	Crop Destruction
Quang Tri	10666	135460	40084	Defoliation
Quang Tri	10566	2850	844	Defoliation
Quang Tri	10367	25500	7555	Defoliation
Quang Tri	10366	3000	899	Defoliation
Quang Tri	10167	3000	899	Defoliation
Quang Tri	10566	500	148	Crop Destruction
Quang Tri	10166	12560	3712	Crop Destruction
Thua Thien	10866	5580	1651	Defoliation

I CORPS - 1967

PROVINCE	PROJECT NUMBER	GALLONS	ACRES SPRAYED	MISSION TYPE
Thua Thien	10767	32100	9504	Defoliation
Thua Thien	10566	18575	5504	Defoliation
Thua Thien	10267	6900	2044	Defoliation
Thua Thien	10166	8010	2369	Crop Destruction
Thua Thien	10866	15930	4709	Crop Destruction
Thua Thien	10566	2000	592	Crop Destruction

PROVINCE	PROJECT NUMBER	GALLONS	ACRES SPRAYED	MISSION TYPE
*Binh Dinh	20167	63869	18900	Defoliation
*Binh Dinh	20167	121770	36031	Crop Destruction
*Binh Dinh	20166	4500	1333	Crop Destruction
*Binh Thuan	20266	97635	28912	Defoliation
*Binh Thuan	20266	17170	5077	Crop Destruction
*Darlac	21167	4100	1214	Crop Destruction
*Khanh Hoa	20766	90215	26694	Defoliation
*Khanh Hoa	20867	13820	4092	Defoliation
*Khanh Hoa	20867	17700	5241	Crop Destruction
*Kontum	20566	13500	3996	Defoliation
*Kontum	20166	101460	30011	Defoliation
*Kontum	20166	19475	5769	Crop Destruction
*Lam Dong	20666	1210	358	Defoliation
*Lam Dong	20967	8950	2651	Defoliation
*Lam Dong	21267	16235	4809	Crop Destruction
*Ninh Thuan	20566	1400	414	Crop Destruction
*Ninh Thuan	20567	4590	1356	Crop Destruction

II CORPS - 1967

PROVINCE	PROJECT NUMBER	GALLONS	ACRES SPRAYED	MISSION TYPE
*Ninh Thuan	20366	7100	2104	Crop Destruction
*Ninh Thuan	20666	37365	11063	Crop Destruction
*Phu Bon	20466	2700	800	Defoliation
*Phu Bon	20366	1600	474	Crop Destruction
*Phu Yen	20367	11050	3273	Defoliation
*Phu Yen	22266	18040	5341	Crop Destruction
*Phu Yen	20367	29585	8764	Crop Destruction
*Pleiku	20467	122910	36387	Defoliation
*Quang Duc	21367	19100	5658	Crop Destruction
*Quang Duc	20667	55350	16399	Defoliation

III CORPS - 1967

PROVINCE	PROJECT NUMBER	GALLONS	ACRES SPRAYED	MISSION TYPE
*Bien Hoa	32066	3600	1067	Defoliation
*Bien Hoa	30566	2790	824	Defoliation
*Bien Hoa	34866	3690	1090	Defoliation
*Bien Hoa	30967	3300	977	Defoliation
*Bien Hoa	31466	30700	9092	Defoliation
*Bien Hoa	38366	6900	2044	Defoliation
*Bien Hoa	30366	150070	44450	Defoliation
*Binh Duong	30566	70050	20747	Defoliation
*Binh Duong	30366	91360	27044	Defoliation
*Binh Duong	34866	22400	6637	Defoliation
*Binh Long	30666	80890	23961	Defoliation
*Binh Tuy	32066	1800	533	Defoliation
*Binh Tuy	31266	50170	14861	Defoliation
*Binh Tuy	30866	10800	3200	Defoliation
*Binh Tuy	31066	177560	52590	Defoliation
*Binh Tuy	31066	22630	6701	Crop Destruction
*Gia Dinh	31666	331990	98348	Defoliation

III CORPS - 1967

PROVINCE	PROJECT NUMBER	GALLONS	ACRES SPRAYED	MISSION TYPE
*Gia Dinh	31666	2000	592	Crop Destruction
*Long An	30367	30700	9095	Defoliation
*Long Khanh	30666	8000	2370	Defoliation
*Long Khanh	30266	4000	1185	Defoliation
*Long Khanh	31366	2500	741	Defoliation
*Long Khanh	30467	21500	6370	Defoliation
*Long Khanh	30667	20375	6799	Defoliation
*Long Khanh	30366	953625	282591	Defoliation**
*Phuoc Long	30167	300795	89112	Defoliation
*Phuoc Long	30366	139815	41410	Defoliation
*Phuoc Tuy	30767	14800	4385	Defoliation
*Phuoc Tuy	30166	102625	30390	Defoliation
*Tay Ninh	30266	227790	66913	Defoliation
*Kontum	30566	2700	800	Defoliation

**Calculated from gallons dispensed at 889ac/1000 gallons.

IV CORPS - 1967

PROVINCE	PROJECT NUMBER	GALLONS	ACRES SPRAYED	MISSION TYPE
*An Xuyen	40366	40200	11909	Defoliation
An Xuyen	40367	5700	1689	Crop Destruction
*An Xuyen	40367	382490	113306	Defoliation
*Bac Lieu	40167	40695	12044	Defoliation
*Khanh Hoa	40767	3000	889	Defoliation
*Kien Hoa	40767	78975	23391	Defoliation
*Kien Phong	40867	9630	2824	Defoliation
*Kien Tuong	40267	7610	2249	Defoliation
*Kien Tuong	40766	18020	5337	Defoliation
*Phong Dinh	40367	10000	2963	Defoliation
*Vinh Binh	40667	2800	829	Defoliation
*Vinh Binh	40166	53290	15786	Defoliation

I CORPS - 1968

PROVINCE	PROJECT NUMBER	GALLONS	ACRES SPRAYED	MISSION TYPE
*Quang Nam	10666	153725	45544	Defoliation
*Quang Nam	10267	2000	592	Defoliation
*Quang Nam	10666	6800	2013	Crop Destruction
*Quang Ngai	10167	37100	10991	Defoliation
*Quang Ngai	10167	8000	2370	Crop Destruction
*Quang Ngai	10166	2900	859	Crop Destruction
*Quang Tin	10766	79400	23527	Defoliation
*Quang Tin	10766	5000	1482	Crop Destruction
*Quang Tri	10367	42795	12677	Defoliation
*Quang Tri	10167	31675	9384	Defoliation
*Quang Tri	10466	45100	13362	Defoliation
*Quang Tri	10666	59100	17512	Defoliation
*Tua Thien	10666	9400	2785	Defoliation
*Thua Thien	10166	6000	1868	Defoliation
*Thua Thien	10167	2000	592	Defoliation
*Thua Thien	10267	34700	10281	Defoliation

I CORPS - 1968

PROVINCE	PROJECT NUMBER	GALLONS	ACRES SPRAYED	MISSION TYPE
*Thua Thien	10566	391225	115905	Defoliation
*Thua Thien	10566	27105	8267	Crop Destruction
*Thua Thien	10568	3000	889	Crop Destruction

II CORPS - 1968

PROVINCE	PROJECT NUMBER	GALLONS	ACRES SPRAYED	MISSION TYPE
*Binh Dinh	20166	3000	889	Defoliation
*Binh Dinh	20568	67600	20300	Defoliation
*Binh Dinh	20167	26950	7984	Defoliation
*Binh Dinh	20568	36300	10754	Crop Destruction
*Binh Thuan	20868	16800	4977	Defoliation
*Binh Thuan	20868	11750	3480	Crop Destruction
*Binh Thuan	20266	7850	2325	Crop Destruction
*Darlac	20867	71150	21083	Defoliation
*Darlac	20668	23050	6830	Defoliation
*Darlac	20668	7500	2222	Crop Destruction
*Khanh Hoa	20867	2000	592	Defoliation
*Khanh Hoa	20168	3000	889	Defoliation
*Khanh Hoa	20766	18800	5570	Defoliation
*Khanh Hoa	20168	19000	5628	Crop Destruction
*Kontum	20166	115800	34311	Defoliation
*Kontum	20168	9000	2667	Defoliation

II CORPS - 1968

PROVINCE	PROJECT NUMBER	GALLONS	ACRES SPRAYED	MISSION TYPE
*Kontum	20167	2900	859	Defoliation
*Lam Dong	20967	20550	6088	Defoliation
*Lam Dong	20468	26450	7837	Crop Destruction
*Ninh Thuan	20666	2150	637	Crop Destruction
*Ninh Thuan	21168	11000	3259	Crop Destruction
*Phu Bon	21068	7000	2163	Crop Destruction
*Phu Yen	20367	18890	5593	Defoliation
*Phu Yen	20768	15000	2665	Defoliation
*Phu Yen	20768	16300	4829	Crop Destruction
*Phu Yen	20367	22000	6517	Crop Destruction
*Pleiku	20467	120520	35712	Defoliation
*Pleiku	20968	5000	1482	Defoliation
*Pleiku	20968	4700	1392	Crop Destruction
*Quang Duc	20667	80025	23710	Defoliation
*Quang Duc	20268	102950	30504	Defoliation
*Quang Duc	20268	3000	889	Crop Destruction

III CORPS - 1968

PROVINCE	PROJECT NUMBER	GALLONS	ACRES SPRAYED	MISSION TYPE
*Bien Hoa	30267	9000	2667	Defoliation
*Bien Hoa	30668	5100	1511	Defoliation
*Bien Hoa	30468	4000	1185	Defoliation
*Bien Hoa	31068	33400	9898	Defoliation
*Bien Hoa	30867	20500	6075	Defoliation
*Bien Hoa	30967	46900	13897	Defoliation
*Bien Hoa	30168	72100	21364	Defoliation
*Binh Duong	30567	65900	19528	Defoliation
*Binh Duong	30868	63950	18951	Defoliation
*Binh Long	30167	5000	1482	Defoliation
*Binh Long	30467	176935	52428	Defoliation
*Binh Tuy	31266	2900	859	Defoliation
*Binh Tuy	31067	5700	1689	Defoliation
*Binh Tuy	31066	69300	20535	Defoliation
*Gia Dinh	31666	298175	88349	Defoliation
*Gia Dinh	31066	6000	1778	Defoliation
*Gia Dinh	31668	3000	889	Defoliation

III CORPS - 1968

PROVINCE	PROJECT NUMBER	GALLONS	ACRES SPRAYED	MISSION TYPE
*Hua Nghia	30568	26200	7764	Defoliation
*Long An	30468	1600	4742	Defoliation
*Long Khanh	30467	41525	12303	Defoliation
*Long Khanh	30366	40800	12090	Defoliation
*Long Khanh	30667	8500	2519	Defoliation
*Long Khanh	30668	101300	30018	Defoliation
*Long Khanh	30268	69000	20447	Defoliation
*Phuoc Long	30366	63800	18905	Defoliation
*Phuoc Long	30166	8000	2370	Defoliation
*Phuoc Long	30368	13000	3853	Defoliation
*Phuoc Long	30168	196350	58182	Defoliation
*Phuoc Long	30167	580175	171925**	Defoliation
*Phuoc Tuy	30267	21600	6401	Defoliation
*Phuoc Tuy	30967	3000	889	Defoliation
*Phuoc Tuy	31066	40750	12076	Defoliation
*Phuoc Tuy	30767	98175	29090	Defoliation
*Tay Ninh	30266	213350	63221	Defoliation

IV CORPS - 1968

PROVINCE	PROJECT NUMBER	GALLONS	ACRES SPRAYED	MISSION TYPE
*An Xuyen	40368	22000	6519	Defoliation
*An Xuyen	40367	104175	30871	Defoliation
*Bac Lieu	40168	42000	12446	Defoliation
*Kien Giang	41068	11000	3259	Defoliation
*Kien Hoa	41467	20750	6149	Defoliation
*Kien Tuong	41567	34950	10357	Defoliation
*Sa Dec	41367	4400	1302	Defoliation
*Vinh Binh	40667	14600	4325	Defoliation
Go Cong	41967	6000	1778	Defoliation

I CORPS - 1969

PROVINCE	PROJECT NUMBER	GALLONS	ACRES SPRAYED	MISSION TYPE
*Quang Nam	10666	24000	7112	Defoliation
*Quang Nam	10369	226725	67170	Defoliation
*Quang Ngai	10167	9000	2667	Defoliation
*Quang Ngai	10568	2700	800	Defoliation
*Quang Ngai	10569	96500	28590	Defoliation
*Quang Ngai	10569	56200	16649	Crop Destruction
*Quang Tin	10766	11000	3259	Defoliation
*Quang Tin	10469	73600	21805	Defoliation
*Quang Tin	10469	29800	8830	Crop Destruction
*Quang Tri	10466	32300	9569	Defoliation
*Quang Tri	10666	37700	11167	Defoliation
*Quang Tri	10169	13700	4059	Defoliation
*Quang Tri	10169	3000	889	Crop Destruction
*Thua Thien	10566	289300	85712	Defoliation
*Thua Thien	10569	13000	3852	Defoliation
*Thua Thien	11069	2000	592	Defoliation
*Thua Thien	10566	8400	2487	Crop Defoliation

II CORPS - 1969

PROVINCE	PROJECT NUMBER	GALLONS	ACRES SPRAYED	MISSION TYPE
*Binh Dinh	20568	55300	16383	Defoliation
*Binh Dinh	20569	53300	15790	Defoliation
*Binh Dinh	20566	3000	889	Crop Destruction
*Binh Dinh	20568	20000	5926	Crop Destruction
Binh Dinh	20569	31700	9391	Crop Destruction
*Darlac	20668	19500	5778	Defoliation
*Darlac	20669	51380	15222	Defoliation
*Darlac	20669	4300	1273	Crop Destruction
*Khanh Hoa	20168	5600	1659	Crop Destruction
*Khanh Hoa	20169	2300	681	Crop Destruction
*Kontum	20166	226500	67114	Defoliation
*Kontum	21269	122000	36137	Defoliation
*Kontum	20269	2600	770	Crop Destruction
*Lam Dong	20469	6500	1926	Defoliation
*Lam Dong	20469	12400	3674	Crop Destruction
*Long Khanh	20669	2000	592	Defoliation
*Ninh Thuan	21168	33400	9897	Defoliation

PROVINCE	PROJECT NUMBER	GALLONS	ACRES SPRAYED	MISSION TYPE
*Ninh Thuan	21168	5100	1511	Crop Destruction
*Phu Yen	20768	11600	3437	Defoliation
*Phu Yen	20768	27000	7998	Crop Destruction
*Pleiku	20968	8000	2371	Defoliation
*Pleiku	20969	6000	1778	Defoliation
*Pleiku	20968	6000	1778	Crop Destruction
*Tuyen Duc	20369	2000	592	Crop Destruction
*Quang Duc	20269	3000	889	Defoliation
*Quang Duc	20268	153000	45339	Defoliation

III CORPS - 1969

PROVINCE	PROJECT NUMBER	GALLONS	ACRES SPRAYED	MISSION TYPE
*Bien Hoa	30168	26000	7704	Defoliation
*Bien Hoa	31068	54600	16181	Defoliation
*Bien Hoa	30169	28000	8297	Defoliation
*Bien Hoa	31069	71000	21037	Defoliation
*Binh Duong	31667	2000	592	Defoliation
*Binh Duong	30868	225783	66905	Defoliation
*Binh Duong	30869	37400	11082	Defoliation
*Binh Long	30467	47900	14194	Defoliation
*Gia Dinh	31669	16000	4740	Defoliation
*Gia Dinh	31666	61800	18313	Defoliation
*Hau Nghia	30568	35600	10549	Defoliation
*Hau Nghia	30569	10000	2964	Defoliation
*Long An	30468	24000	7113	Defoliation
*Long An	30469	50200	14876	Defoliation
*Long Khanh	30669	83700	24801	Defoliation
*Phuoc Long	30168	465450	137926	Defoliation

III CORPS - 1969

PROVINCE	PROJECT NUMBER	GALLONS	ACRES SPRAYED	MISSION TYPE
*Phuoc Long	30169	691400	204874	Defoliation
*Phuoc Long	30368	23000	6815	Defoliation
*Tay Ninh	30368	142600	42255	Defoliation
*Tay Ninh	30369	14600	4327	Defoliation
*Tay Ninh	30769	18900	5600	Defoliation

IV CORPS - 1969

PROVINCE	PROJECT NUMBER	GALLONS	ACRES SPRAYED	MISSION TYPE
An Xuyen	43469	7000	2074	Defoliation
*An Xuyen	40368	57800	17127	Defoliation
Bac Lieu	40168	21000	6223	Defoliation
*Chuong Thien	41069	9600	2844	Defoliation
*Kien Giang	41669	12000	3555	Defoliation
*Kien Hoa	41368	8000	2371	Defoliation
*Kien Hoa	43268	18000	5334	Defoliation
*Kien Tuong	42668	64000	18966	Defoliation
*Phong Dinh	43568	16000	4741	Defoliation
*Vinh Binh	41368	85000	25189	Defoliation

I CORPS - 1970

PROVINCE	PROJECT NUMBER	GALLONS	ACRES SPRAYED	MISSION TYPE
*Quang Nam	10369	7700	2281	Defoliation
*Quang Ngai	10569	12100	3585	Crop Destruction
*Quang Tin	10469	6700	1985	Defoliation
*Quang Tin	10469	6000	1778	Crop Destruction
*Quang Tri	10169	1700	503	Defoliation
*Thua Thien	10566	27100	8028	Defoliation
*Thua Thien	10566	5100	1511	Crop Destruction

II CORPS - 1970

PROVINCE	PROJECT NUMBER	GALLONS	ACRES SPRAYED	MISSION TYPE
*Binh Dinh	20569	3600	1066	Crop Destruction
*Binh Dinh	20570	13800	4089	Crop Destruction
*Darlac	20669	1800	533	Defoliation
*Darlac	20669	4500	1333	Crop Destruction
*Darlac	20670	10480	3103	Crop Destruction
*Khanh Hoa	20170	20700	6133	Crop Destruction
*Kontum	21269	252850	74914	Defoliation
*Kontum	21269	4200	1244	Crop Destruction
*Lam Dong	20469	4000	1185	Crop Destruction
*Ninh Thuan	21169	2200	652	Defoliation
*Ninh Thuan	21169	4600	1362	Crop Destruction
*Ninh Thuan	21170	3350	991	Crop Destruction
*Phu Bon	21069	8300	2458	Crop Destruction
*Phu Yen	20769	6000	1776	Defoliation
*Phu Yen	20769	2200	651	Crop Destruction

II CORPS - 1970

PROVINCE	PROJECT NUMBER	GALLONS	ACRES SPRAYED	MISSION TYPE
*Pleiku	20969	42600	12620	Defoliation
*Pleiku	20970	6000	1778	Defoliation
Quang Duc	20269	5800	1718	Crop Destruction
Tuyen Duc	20369	2500	741	Crop Destruction

III CORPS - 1970

PROVINCE	PROJECT NUMBER	GALLONS	ACRES SPRAYED	MISSION TYPE
*Bien Hoa	31069	10600	3139	Defoliation
*Binh Duong	30869	64000	18964	Defoliation
*Binh Tuy	30170	3400	1007	Crop Destruction
*Phuoc Long	30169	138200	40946	Defoliation
*Phuoc Long	30270	69230	20510	Defoliation
Phuoc Long	30770	31800	9423	Defoliation

IV CORPS - 1970

PROVINCE	PROJECT NUMBER	GALLONS	ACRES SPRAYED	MISSION TYPE
*An Xuyen	43469	61500	18223	Defoliation
*Kien Giang	43869	12000	3556	Defoliation

II CORPS - 1971

PROVINCE	PROJECT NUMBER	GALLONS	ACRES SPRAYED	MISSION TYPE
Ninh Thuan	21170	1900	563	Crop Destruction

APPENDIX D

HERBICIDE SORTIES IN LAOS

1965 - 1969

The information in this Appendix was extracted from the MACV J3 Surface Operations Division computer bank.

HERBICIDE OPERATIONS IN LAOS

Date	Project Number	Area Sprayed in Hectares*	Gallons Dispensed	Herbicide
Dec 1965	20W	6,120	41,050	Orange
Jan 1966	20W	9,255	59,400	Orange
Feb 1966	20W	9,590	62,150	Orange
Mar 1966	20W	4,855	29,300	Orange
Apr 1966	20W	3,360	21,700	Orange
May 1966	20W	3,560	23,000	Orange
Jun 1966	20W	3,515	12,700	Orange
Jul 1966	20W	4,010	26,000	Orange
Aug 1966	20W	3,425	22,100	Orange
Sep 1966	20W	620	4,000	Orange
	2W	1,180	7,600	Orange
Oct 1966	20W	1,400	9,000	White
	2W	700	4,500	White
Nov 1966	20W	2,910	20,010	White
	20W	600	3,600	Orange
Dec 1966	20W	2,100	12,600	White
Jan 1967	20W	1,500	9,000	White
	20W	1,700	10,300	Orange
Feb 1967	20W	1,500	9,000	Orange
Mar 1967	20W	450	2,790	Orange
Oct 1968	---	720	6,000	Orange
Nov 1968	---	960	8,000	Blue
Dec 1968	---	360	2,700	Orange
Feb 1969	---	840	7,000	Orange
Sep 1969	---	762	6,350	Blue

*Note: 2.471 acres = 1 hectare

FOOTNOTES

CHAPTER I

1. (U) Major James S. Kelly, "Where Have all the Ranch Hands Gone?", Office of Information, 35th Tactical Fighter Wing (PACAF), Phan Rang AB, 1971

2. (S) History 315th Tactical Airlift Wing, Phan Rang AB, Vietnam, July - September 1969

3. (S) History 315th Tactical Airlift Wing, Phan Rang AB, Vietnam, 1 January - 31 March 1971

4. (S) Interview, topic: Herbicide Operations. With Major S. O. Swanson, Operations Officer, A Flight, 310th TAS by Captain James R. Clary, at Phan Rang AB, RVN, 21 May 1971

CHAPTER II

5. (S) Report, subj: "Herbicide Operations in the Republic of Vietnam," undated (Hereafter cited as Herbicide Operations Report)

6. (S) Report, subj: "TAC Aerial Spray Flight Operations in Southeast Asia, 1961-1964," undated (Hereafter cited as TAC Aerial Spray Flight Report)

7. (S) Herbicide Operations Report. See also TAC Aerial Spray Flight Report

8. (S) Draft Report, subj: Defoliation and Ranch Hand in the Republic of South Vietnam, 1 July 1965 (Hereafter cited as Defoliation and Ranch Hand Report)

9. (S) Herbicide Operations Report

10. (TS) History USMACV 1964; material extracted is (S).

11. (S) Defoliation and Ranch Hand Report
    TAC Aerial Spray Flight Report

12. (S) <u>Ibid</u>

13. (S) Ibid

14. (TS) History USMACV 1964; material extracted is (S)

15. (S) CHECO Report, subject: "Herbicide Operations in Southeast Asia, July 1961 - June 1967," Hq PACAF

16. (S) TAC Aerial Spray Flight Report

17. (S) Ibid

18. (S) Ibid

19. (S) Ibid

20. (S) Herbicide Operations Report

21. (S) Defoliation and Ranch Hand Report

22. (S) Report, subj: "Evaluation of Crop Destruction in RVN," 1 July 1966, MACV J3-09 files

    (S) Defoliation and Ranch Hand Report

23. (S) Msg COMUSMACV to CINCPAC, subj: Herbicide Operations, 11602Z January 1967

24. (S) Summary of Defoliation Operations 1 January 1965 to 8 March 1965, undated

    (S) Defoliation and Ranch Hand Report

25. (S) Defoliation and Ranch Hand Report

26. (U) Report, subj: "Operation Sherwood Forest," undated in CHECO files

    (S) Defoliation and Ranch Hand Report

    (S) Summary of Defoliation Operations 1 January 1965 to 8 March 1965, undated

27. (S) Defoliation and Ranch Hand Report

    (S) Report, subj: "Evaluation of Crop Destruction in RVN," 1 July 1966, MACV J3-09 files

28. (S)   <u>Ibid</u>

29. (S)   Summary of Defoliation Operations from 8 March to 30 June 1965, undated

30. (S)   Folder, Project 2-28 Herbicide Operations MACV J3-09

31. (S)   Folder, Project 20-58 Herbicide Operations MACV J3-09

32. (S)   Folder, Project 20-55 Herbicide Operations MACV J3-09

33. (S)   Folder, Project 20-68 Herbicide Operations MACV J3-09

34. (S)   Report, subj: "Defoliation Operations in Laos," 1 January 1966

    (TS) Project CHECO Report, subj: "Tiger Hound," September 1966, extracted material is Secret

35. (TS) <u>Ibid</u>

36. (S)   Hq USMACV Monthly Evaluation Report, January 1966

37. (S)   Hq USMACV Monthly Evaluation Report, February 1966

38. (S)   Folder, Project 20-69 Herbicide Operations MACV J3-09

    (TS) Hq USMACV Briefing for Major General C. E. Hutchins, 18 March 1966, subj: Herbicide Operations. Material extracted is Secret

39. (S)   Hq USMACV Monthly Evaluation Report, March 1966

40. (S)   Hq USMACV Monthly Evaluation Report, April 1966

41. (C)   USMACV J3 Surface Operations Division, Herbicide Operations Report/Computer Bank, May 1971

42. (S)   Interview, topic: Herbicide Operations. With Lieutenant Colonel R. Dennis, Commander, 12th ACS, by Captain Charles V. Collins, Project CHECO, 1967

43. (S)   Interview, topic: Herbicide Operations. With Captain W. Marchaleck, Targeting Officer, 12th ACS by Captain Charles V. Collins, Project CHECO, 1967

44. (S)   <u>Ibid</u>

45. (S)   Msg COMUSMACV to CINCPAC, subj: Herbicide Operations, 031105Z April 1966

46. (U)   Ranch Hand Briefing Notes, Herbicide Operations, undated, MACV J3-09 files

47. (S)   Interview, topic: Herbicide Operations. With Captain W. Marshaleck, Targeting Officer, 12th ACS, by Captain Charles V. Collins, Project CHECO, 1967

48. (S)   <u>Ibid</u>

    (S)   Defoliation Operations in Southeast Asia, Project CORONA HARVEST, March 1970

49. (S)   Msg, 7AF to CINCPAC, subj: Herbicide Operations, 060535Z April 1967

50. (S)   Pink Rose Test Plan, 26 December 1966

    (S)   Final Report of the Operational Evaluation of Project Pink Rose, 5 May 1967

51. (S)   Final Report of the Operational Evaluation of Project Pink Rose, 5 May 1967

52. (S)   <u>Ibid</u>

53. (S)   TAC Airlift Performance Analysis - Southeast Asia, May 1967, MACV J3-09

    (S)   Interview, topic: Herbicide Operations. With Lieutenant Colonel R. Dennis, Commander, 12th ACS, by Captain Charles V. Collins, Project CHECO, 1967

54. (S)   Msg, CGIFFORCEV to UUMSE/COMUSMACV-COC7, subject: Herbicide Operations, 191019Z July 1967

55. (S)   Msg, 366th CSG to RUEDHQA/CSAF, subject: Herbicide Operations, 041119Z July 1967

CHAPTER III

56. (S) CHECO Report, subject: "The War in Vietnam, January-June 1967," Hq PACAF, dated 28 April 1968

57. (S) Commander's Operation Command Book, July 1966 - July 1967, Hq 7th Air Force

58. (S) Project CORONA HARVEST Special Report "Defoliation Operations in Southeast Asia," Hq AU, March 1970

59. (S) Study, subject: "Ranch Hand Study" 834th Air Division, 12 September 1967

60. (C) Russel Betts and Frank Denton, "An Evaluation of Chemical Crop Destruction Operations in Vietnam," Rand Corporation, October 1967

61. (S) W. F. Warren, L. L. Henry and R. D. Johnson, "Crop Destruction in RVN during CY 67," dated 23 December 1967 (Scientific Advisory Group Working Paper No. 20-67)

62. (C) Msg, 7th AF to CSAF, subj: "Herbicide Crop Destruction Operations in SVN," reproduced in supplement to History 7th Air Force 1 July - 31 December 1967

63. (S) 7th Air Force History, 1 July - 31 December 1967, Volume I Narrative

64. (C) Msg, 834th AD to 315th ACW, subject: Herbicide Operations dated 11 January 1968 (315th SOW correspondence file, Air University Archives CH-5-5-1)

    (S) Ltr, subject: Modification Requirements for UC-123K Aircraft, Hq USAF, 27 May 1968 (in file subject: Improved Defoliation Capability (UC-123K aircraft) May-June 1968, Air University Archives CH-4-14-25)

65. (S) Report on Herbicide Policy Review, dated 28 August 1968, American Embassy, Saigon, RVN

    (S) Msg, COMUSMACV to CINCPAC, subject: Effectiveness of Herbicide Operations, 30 August 1968 (Air University Archives CH-5-4-19)

66. (S) Project CORONA HARVEST Special Report, subject: Defoliation Operations in Southeast Asia, Hq AU, March 1970

67. (S) USMACV Year-End Review of Vietnam - 1968 (Air University Archives CH-16-1-9)

    (S) 834th Air Division Reports, subject: Tactical Airlift Performance and Accomplishments, June 1968 and July 1969

68. (S) <u>Ibid</u>

69. (S) 834th Air Division Report, subject: Tactical Airlift Performance and Accomplishments, Southeast Asia, June 1970

70. (S) Msg, COMUSMACV to 7th AF, subject: Herbicide Operations, 060305Z January 1970

    (S) Msg, COMUSMACV to 7th AF, subject: Herbicide Operations, 061111Z January 1970

71. (S) Msg, CSAF to CINCPAC, subject: Herbicide Operations, 022006Z February 1970

72. (S) Msg, CINCPAC to COMUSMACV, subject: Herbicide Operations, 070333Z March 1970

73. (S) CINCPACAF to CSAF, subject: Herbicide Operations, 060719Z March 1970

74. (S) Msg, CSAF to CINCPAC/COMUSMACV, subject: Herbicide Operations, 31200Z March 1970

    (S) 834th Air Division Report, subject: Tactical Airlift Performance and Accomplishments, Southeast Asia, October 1970

75. (S) Msg, COMUSMACV to 7th AF, subject: Herbicide Operations, 200015Z March 1970

76. (C) Msg, 7th AF to 12th SOS, subject: Herbicide Operations, 061245Z April 1970

77. (S) 315th Tactical Airlift Wing History, April - June 1970

78. (S) Msg, 7th AF to 315th TAWg, subject: Herbicide Operations, 191100Z April 1970

79. (S)　Msg, COMUSMACV to 7th AF, subject: Herbicide Operations, 170300Z April 1970

    (S)　315th Tactical Airlift Wing History, April - June 1970

    (S)　Appendix A, this report

80. (S)　315th Tactical Airlift Wing History, April - June 1970

81. (S)　834th Air Division Report, subject: Tactical Airlift Performance and Accomplishments, Southeast Asia, October 1970

82. (S)　Msg, 7th AF to 12th SOS, subject: Herbicide Operations, 091205Z May 1970

83. (S)　315th Tactical Airlift Wing History, April - June 1970

84. (S)　Ibid

85. (C)　Msg, 7th AF to 315th TAWg, subject: Herbicide Operations, 291120Z June 1970

    (S)　315th Tactical Airlift Wing History, April - June 1970

86. (S)　315th Tactical Airlift Wing History, April - June 1970

    (S)　315th Tactical Airlift Wing History, July - September 1970

87. (S)　Ibid

88. (S)　315th Tactical Airlift Wing History, July - September 1970

89. (S)　Msg, COMUSMACV to 7th AF, subject: Herbicide Operations, 170709Z July 1970

90. (S)　315th Tactical Airlift Wing History, July - September 1970

91. (S)　315th Tactical Airlift Wing History, July - September 1970

    (S)　Interview, topic: Herbicide Operations. With Major Stanley O. Swanson, Operations Officer, 310th TAS by Captain James R. Clary at Phan Rang AB, 21 May 1971

92. (S)　315th Tactical Airlift Wing History, July - September 1970

93. (S)　Ibid

94. (S) 315th Tactical Airlift Wing History, July - September 1970

    (S) Command Correspondence Staff Summary Sheet, subject: Herbicide Operations, dated 14 September 1970

95. (S) Interview, topic: Herbicide Operations. With Major Stanley O. Swanson, Operations Officer, 310th TAS by Captain James R. Clary at Phan Rang AB, 21 May 1971

96. (S) CINCPAC Scientific Advisory Group Working Paper Number 5-70, subject: Interdiction Operations in SEA, 26 May 1970

    (S) Work Copy of Cost Calculations and Sources for Herbicide Operations by Major Duckworth, Hq 7th AF (DOAT), undated

97. (S) Interview, topic: Herbicide Operations. With Major Robert Markham, Targeting Officer, 310th TAS by Captain James R. Clary, at Phan Rang AB, 22 May 1971

98. (S) Msg, COMUSMACV to 7th AF, subject: Herbicide Operations, 170515Z October 1970

99. (S) Appendix A, this report

100. (S) Msg, COMUSMACV to 7th AF, subject: Herbicide Operations, 210904Z November 1970

101. (S) Msg, SAAMA (Kelly AFB, Texas) to 7th AF, subject: Herbicide Operations, 042145Z December 1970

102. (S) 310th Tactical Airlift Squadron A Flight History, 1 - 31 January 1971

103. (S) Msg, COMUSMACV to 834th Air Division, subject: Herbicide Operations, 271133Z January 1971

104. (S) 310th Tactical Airlift Squadron A Flight History, 1 - 31 January 1971

CHAPTER IV

105. (U) P. R. Ehrlich, _Population, Resources, Environment_, W. H. Freeman and Company, 1970

106. (U) H. M. Hull, _Herbicide Handbook of the Weed Society of America_, Humphrey Press, Geneva, New York, 1967

107. (U) F. H. Tschirley, Science 163 (3869), 779-786, 1969

108. (U) J. E. McDonald, Weather 17:1, 1962

109. (U) J. P. Decker, Plant Physiology, 37:393, 1962

110. (U) H. L. Ohman and R. L. Pratt, The Daytime Influence of Irrigation Upon Desert Humidities, Technical Report Number EP-35, U.S. Army Quartermaster R&D Command, 1956

111. (U) F. H. Tschirley, Science 163 (3869), 779-786, 1969

    (U) Tropical Silviculture 1:129, 1958

112. (U) T. W. McKinley, The Forests of Free Vietnam, Ministry of Agriculture, Saigon, 1957

APPENDIX A

113. (S) Minutes - Meeting of Defoliants Anti-Crop Systems Subcommittee of the JTCG/CB, 8-9 December 1970, dated 22 January 1971, published by Air Force Armament Laboratory (AFSC), Eglin AFB, Florida. (Extracted information is unclassified, Limited Official Use)

114. (U) Letter, Fort Dettrick, Maryland, Plant Sciences Laboratory 20 November 1970, summarizing experimental studies on Range C-52A

115. (U) AAS Vietnam Herbicide Assessment Conference, 14-21 June 1970, National Academy of Sciences, Woods Hole, Massachusettes, Trip Report by Dr. C. E. Minarik

116. (U) Toxicity of Herbicides in Use in Vietnam, Dr. C. E. Minarik, Director Plant Science Laboratory, Dr. R. A. Darrow, Chief, Plant Physiology Division, Department of the Army, Fort Dettrick, Maryland, April 1968

117. (U) Persistence of Herbicides in Soil and Water by Dr. C. E. Minarik, Director Plant Sciences Laboratory, Dr. R. A. Darrow, Chief, Plant Physiology Division, Department of the Army, Fort Dettrick, Maryland, 1968 April 1968

118. (U) Panel Session, American Association for the Advancement of Science, 29 December 1970, subject: Implications of Continued Military Use of Herbicides in SEA, comments by Dr. Fred H. Tschirley, Agricultural Research Service, U.S. Department of Agriculture

APPENDIX B

119. (S) 834th Air Division Report, subject: Tactical Airlift Performance and Accomplishments, Southeast Asia, June 1968

120. (S) <u>Ibid</u>

    (S) 834th Air Division Report, subject: Tactical Airlift Performance and Accomplishments, Southeast Asia, July 1969

121. (S) 834th Air Division Reports, subject: Tactical Airlift Performance and Accomplishments, Southeast Asia, June 1970 and July 1969

122. (S) 834th Air Division Reports, subject: Tactical Airlift Performance and Accomplishments, Southeast Asia, October 1970 and March 1971

123. (S) 834th Air Division Reports, subject: Tactical Airlift Performance and Accomplishments, Southeast Asia, March 1971

GLOSSARY

A/A 45Y-1 Dispensing System		Improved herbicide dispensing system installed in UC-123K aircraft from mid-1965
ACS		Air Commando Squadron
AD		Air Division
Arc Light	(S)	B-52 operations in SEA. Example of typical 1969 operations: Operations include ten missions daily of six aircraft per mission, with two cells of three aircraft per mission from the following locations: Five missions from U-Tapao, three missions from Guam and two missions from Kadena (TACPAL)
Blue		Herbicide composed of cacodylic acid being effective against narrow leaf vegetation, notably crops
CBU		Cluster Bomb Unit
CDTC/RVNAF		Chemical Division Test Center/Republic of Vietnam Air Force
CHMAAGV		Chief, Military Assistance Advisory Group, Vietnam
CINCPAC		Commander-in-Chief, Pacific
CINCPACAF		Commander-in-Chief, Pacific Air Forces
COMUSMACV		Commander, United States Military Assistance Command, Vietnam
CSAF		Chief of Staff, United States Air Force

DECCA		Tactical Air Positioning System
Dioxin		Trace contaminant in orange herbicide, believed to have mutagenic properties
DMZ		Demilitarized Zone separating North and South Vietnam
DoD		Department of Defense
FAC		Forward Air Controller. As utilized in South Vietnam, an officer rated pilot member of the Tactical Air Control Party (TACP) who, from a forward airborne position, controls strike aircraft engaged in close air support (CAS) of ground troops; also used to control strike aircraft engaged in direct air support and targets of opportunity operations
Farmgate	(S)	Replaced shortlived Jungle Jim as covert USAF mission to train VNAF personnel beginning in December 1961
GVN		Government of South Vietnam
Hot Tip I/Hot Tip II		Jungle burning project in South Vietnam in Chu Phong Mountain Area
NVA		North Vietnamese Army
MACV		Military Assistance Command, Vietnam
MC-1 Dispenser		Early herbicide dispensing system, prior to 1966 for C-123 aircraft
Mountain Ranch		Code name for herbicide unit operating at Da Nang AB, Vietnam for operations in MR I
Orange		Herbicide comprised of 2,4-D and 2,4,5-T, effective against broadleaf vegetation, used for defoliation operations
OSD		Office of the Secretary of Defense

Project Pink Rose		Jungle burning project, using herbicides and incendiary bombs in War Zones C and D, running from late 1966 to April 1967. The project was unsuccessful.
Psyops		Psychological operations which include psychological warfare and, in addition, encompass those political, military, economic and ideological actions planned and conducted to create in neutral or friendly foreign groups, the emotions, attitude or behavior to support the achievement of national objectives
Psywar		Psychological Warfare
Ranch Hand		Code name for the unit engaged in herbicide operations
RVN		Republic of Vietnam
SASF		Special Aerial Spray Flight, normally assigned to spraying insecticide in disease control programs in the United States and around the world; later detailed to dispense herbicide in Vietnam
SEA		Southeast Asia
Project Sherwood Forest	(S)	Attempt to defoliate and burn the Boi Loi Woods, north of Saigon. Fire apparently created a thunderstorm which put out the fire
Slash and Burn		Clearing, burning of jungle areas for cultivation. A normal Montagnard technique, adopted by the Viet Cong and NVA to make it harder for USAF/VNAF crews to destroy the crops
SOS		Special Operations Squadron
Steel Tiger	(S)	Geographic area in southern Laos designated by 7AF to facilitate planning and operations

Swamp Fox		Defoliation missions against VC strongholds in Bac Lieu, Ba Xuyen and Vinh Binh Provinces, conducted from 30 April - 25 May 1965
TACC		Tactical Air Control Center (in-country)
TAS		Tactical Airlift Squadron
TAWg		Tactical Airlift Wing
Teratogenic		Capability for producing defects, abnormalities, or monstrosities, especially in humans. Attributed to pure concentrations of dioxin, a trace contaminant of herbicide Orange
Tiger Hound	(S)	Southern Steel Tiger, south of 17 degrees north employing FACs, 6 December 1965 - 14 November 1968. Redesignated Steel Tiger South, with northern boundary moved somewhat south. The employment of FACs represented an innovation in the conduct of the air war in Laos (to conduct interdiction). Superseded by 7AF OPLAN 512-70.
Trail Dust		Code name for herbicide operations in Southeast Asia
VC		Viet Cong
VJGS		Vietnamese Joint General Staff
VNAF		South Vietnamese Air Force
War Zone C		Viet Cong redoubt northwest of Saigon, roughly encompassing Tay Ninh Province
White		Herbicide comprised of 2,4-D and picloram, effective against broadleaf vegetation
Project Yankee		Crop denial missions in the An Loa Valley of Binh Dinh Province

Project Pink Rose		Jungle burning project, using herbicides and incendiary bombs in War Zones C and D, running from late 1966 to April 1967. The project was unsuccessful.
Psyops		Psychological operations which include psychological warfare and, in addition, encompass those political, military, economic and ideological actions planned and conducted to create in neutral or friendly foreign groups, the emotions, attitude or behavior to support the achievement of national objectives
Psywar		Psychological Warfare
Ranch Hand		Code name for the unit engaged in herbicide operations
RVN		Republic of Vietnam
SASF		Special Aerial Spray Flight, normally assigned to spraying insecticide in disease control programs in the United States and around the world; later detailed to dispense herbicide in Vietnam
SEA		Southeast Asia
Project Sherwood Forest	(S)	Attempt to defoliate and burn the Boi Loi Woods, north of Saigon. Fire apparently created a thunderstorm which put out the fire
Slash and Burn		Clearing, burning of jungle areas for cultivation. A normal Montagnard technique, adopted by the Viet Cong and NVA to make it harder for USAF/VNAF crews to destroy the crops
SOS		Special Operations Squadron
Steel Tiger	(S)	Geographic area in southern Laos designated by 7AF to facilitate planning and operations

Swamp Fox		Defoliation missions against VC strongholds in Bac Lieu, Ba Xuyen and Vinh Binh Provinces, conducted from 30 April - 25 May 1965
TACC		Tactical Air Control Center (in-country)
TAS		Tactical Airlift Squadron
TAWg		Tactical Airlift Wing
Teratogenic		Capability for producing defects, abnormalities, or monstrosities, especially in humans. Attributed to pure concentrations of dioxin, a trace contaminant of herbicide Orange
Tiger Hound	(S)	Southern Steel Tiger, south of 17 degrees north employing FACs, 6 December 1965 - 14 November 1968. Redesignated Steel Tiger South, with northern boundary moved somewhat south. The employment of FACs represented an innovation in the conduct of the air war in Laos (to conduct interdiction). Superseded by 7AF OPLAN 512-70.
Trail Dust		Code name for herbicide operations in Southeast Asia
VC		Viet Cong
VJGS		Vietnamese Joint General Staff
VNAF		South Vietnamese Air Force
War Zone C		Viet Cong redoubt northwest of Saigon, roughly encompassing Tay Ninh Province
White		Herbicide comprised of 2,4-D and picloram, effective against broadleaf vegetation
Project Yankee		Crop denial missions in the An Loa Valley of Binh Dinh Province

RESEARCH NOTE

Footnotes Numbers 5 to 55 are original document references cited in CHECO Southeast Asia Report, subj: Herbicide Operations in Southeast Asia, July 1961 - June 1967, from which the Herbicide Review was extracted, excepting references to CHECO Report on Tiger Hound and CORONA HARVEST Report on Defoliation Operations in Southeast Asia.

www.ingramcontent.com/pod-product-compliance
Lightning Source LLC
Chambersburg PA
CBHW080548170426
43195CB00016B/2717